TRACING INCA TRAILS

TRACING
INCA
TRAILS

An Adventure in the Andes

EDDY ANCINAS

SHE WRITES PRESS

Published 2022
Printed in the United States of America
Print ISBN: 978-1-64742-277-6
E-ISBN: 978-1-64742-278-3
Library of Congress Control Number: 2022908727

For information, address:
She Writes Press
1569 Solano Ave #546
Berkeley, CA 94707

Interior design by Tabitha Lahr
All interior photos are courtesy of the author.

She Writes Press is a division of SparkPoint Studio, LLC.

For my Children
Marcos, Carmen and René
Exploring the world with you and sharing its
many wonders has given me profound happiness.

And a wish for my Grandchildren
Be curious—Read—Embrace the unknown
And the gifts of travel will reward you in
ways you never imagined.

INTRODUCTION

▼▼▼▼▼▼▼▼▼▼▼▼▼▼▼

When I returned from Perú in 1986, I knew I had done something extraordinary. Together with two friends and a group of fellow travelers, I had ridden a horse for seven days over the Andes and down to a jungle outpost where a train would be waiting to take us to Machu Picchu—a much anticipated destination. Along the way, one of my friends fell from her horse resulting in injuries. Two pack mules carrying our gear tumbled from the trail into a river. When we finally reached the train station, we learned there was a strike—no train to Machu Picchu, no way to get back to Cusco. What we thought was the end of our journey was the beginning of a new one. Setting off late in the afternoon along the railroad tracks, on foot and on horseback, we had no idea how we would get back over the Andes to Cusco.

During this adventure, as each of us responded to moments of terror and elation, distress and discovery, we found individual strengths and vulnerabilities we didn't know we had. Perú, with its great mountains and mysteries, was the perfect setting for a true adventure travel book. But who would read it? For months, friends and family had been telling me, *I can't believe you did that,* and *Glad you did it, and I don't have to,* or *I'd rather read about it than do it.*

The following summer, at the 1987 Squaw Valley Community of Writers Conference, Richard Rhinehart (author, journalist, historian and lecturer at the U.C. Graduate School of Journalism) was asked by a panel of agents and editors, "What's selling in bookstores today?" When I heard his answer, *non-fiction, travel narratives, especially by women,*" I thought, "Wow! Do I have a story." I bought my first computer and started writing.

Now, twenty-four years later, after numerous revisions interspersed with long abandonment in a drawer, I decided to re-visit the manuscript and meet the challenge of re-writing the story for today's audience. Convinced that love of adventure and the joy of discovery have no time frame, I returned to my manuscript and to Perú—still in love with the country and grateful for the lessons I learned along the Inca trails, where the mysteries of ancient civilizations continue to confound and delight travelers from around the world.

Chapter One

CALLE LORETO

▼▼▼▼▼▼▼▼▼▼▼▼▼▼▼

"There's not a single door on this street," said my father.
"It's the same as when the Incas were here."
This street was like the walls carved out by rivers,
between which passes no one but the waters.
—From *Los Rios Profundos (Deep Rivers)*
By José María Arguedas, on visiting Cusco
as a boy with his father

The Calle Loreto runs in a straight line from the Coricancha (Temple of the Sun) to the Plaza de Armas in the center of Cusco. Flanked on one side by the wall of the Palace of Huayna Capac, last king of the Incas, and on the other by the wall of Acllahuasi (Temple of the Chosen Women), it was the royal way of the Inca.

Today, it is the way of three women on their way to the plaza. Walking single file down the narrow street, we stop to look at a block-long Inca wall. I reach out to the largest stone and run my fingers around its twelve-sided perimeter, searching for a crack

Calle Loreto

where one stone meets the next. Stones of all shapes and sizes form a seamless granite patchwork—carved, carried, and constructed into walls and palaces by the Incas four hundred years ago.

Kate crosses the street to stand with her back against the opposite wall, camera aimed for a wide-angle shot. Her soft gray hair, gathered loosely in an antique silver barrette, is the same blend of grays as the weathered stones. "Just think, if we were the 'Chosen Women,' we would live here," she says.

"The Inca would never choose you," I say, laughing. "You are way too independent."

Kate, a competent and caring nurse, possesses an air of self-confidence that inspires trust and hope in those of us who believe she can cure our ills, mend our broken limbs, and console us in times of pain or misfortune. Through sickness, injuries and recoveries, raising children, starting businesses, and building houses, we have shared our expectations, disappointments, and successes. We have been friends for twenty years, and like most of her friends, I have always counted on Kate for an opinion on life's challenges: be they physical, psychological, spiritual, political, or nonexistent. Living and working in our ski resort community and an active life of skiing, hiking, and coping with the elements has kept her slender, strong, and fit, but the combination of weather, Irish skin, and the cares of her profession have lined her face beyond her sixty years.

"We'd have been cast out by now," Tricia says, stepping resolutely onto the narrow stone sidewalk. "Too old to conceive the next Inca . . . but they might have kept us for our great wisdom." She bends her petite frame backwards to gaze up at the wall, grabbing the dark glasses that hold her strawberry blond hair in place.

Tricia and Kate have been friends for longer than I have known either of them, but over the past five years of our friendship, Tricia and I have found much in common, and a shared attraction to anything foreign, especially Latin, guaranteed her interest in Peru.

Curious about the world and its inhabitants, Tricia relishes each new discovery—whether in a book, a museum, a café, or on the street. She is an artist and a collector, and her home reflects thirty years of travel and changing tastes. Bold, color-filled paintings (hers and others) speak of joy and optimism in shades of purple, pink, and orange. Curious little statues and ceramic bowls occupy every level surface—ledge, table, windowsill. Woven textiles, draped over chairs and couches, add to the ethnic mélange. Creator and owner of a gift shop appropriately called "Design Madness," Tricia has passed from her Indian phase of the '60s, to Morocco in the '70s, pre-Columbian Mexico and Mesoamerica in the '80s. Peru is next.

SIX MONTHS AGO, ON A SNOWY NIGHT in January 1984, Kate, Tricia, and their husbands came to my house to see slides of Peru taken by a friend, Bill Roberson, who hoped my husband, Osvaldo, and I might join him on his next trip to Peru. Across the screen in brilliant Kodachrome flashed noble Indian faces, Inca walls, colorful markets, and close-ups of women carrying snotty-nosed babies on their backs.

Kate wanted to know about respiratory diseases, hygiene, medical care, housing, sanitation, and survival in the high altitude. Bill had little information.

When the walls of Machu Picchu filled the screen, Tricia, who had lived in Mexico and studied archeology, said, "I'd give anything to see that. Before I die, I must see that."

"That looks like Nepal," Kate's husband commented when the white brilliance of an enormous mountain illuminated the living room and cast an incandescent pallor on our faces.

"It's the second highest mountain in Peru: 25,574 feet," Bill replied.

"What's its name?" I asked.

"Salcantay. It means 'The Wild One' in Quechua."

Another photo showed a waterfall of snow and debris dropping into a chasm at the bottom of the screen. "If you're lucky," Bill continued, "you'll see a glacier let loose. It's an awesome sight. This is the second day of the horseback ride across the Andes. After we ride over a fifteen-thousand-foot pass, we camp on the other side of Salcantay, and you can hear the glaciers sliding off during the night."

The vision of that mountain—its serene beauty and its potential violence—held an attraction for me that I could neither explain nor escape. My ancestors were pioneers, my father and his father mountaineers. Did I inherit the need to explore the unknown, to take physical risk for spiritual reward—or is it a basic need in every human being?

I had been to Peru twenty years ago. When Osvaldo and I were first married, we took a freighter down the West Coast of South America on our way to his hometown in Argentina, stopping in Callao, the port town of Lima. I remember a sullen city, sprawling inward from the sea under a leaden sky. Little gangster cars raced through traffic lights on cobblestone streets. Our taxi lacked a door but offered a hole in the floor where you could watch the street go by. In all our subsequent trips to Argentina, we never went beyond the llama rugs and pisco bottles in the souvenir shop of the Lima airport. Like most people, I knew about Machu Picchu, but I didn't know about Salcantay—or about Peru.

AT THE END OF CALLE LORETO, the inward sloping wall of the Temple of the Chosen Women rounds the corner on to the Plaza de Armas, where all the ancient roads of the Incas converge. Here, in the center of Tawantinsuyu, the four corners of the universe, the Incas built their holy city of gilded temples, fountains, gardens, and palaces. From here they went north to Ecuador, south to Chile and Argentina, and conquered tribes in the mountains, the jungles, and along the coast.

With Cusco as their capitol, the Incas organized and administered their land for the common good. United by a common language, Quechua, and a common god, Inti (the sun), the Inca Empire stretched from Santiago, Chile, in the south, to the border between Ecuador and Columbia in the north, and from the Pacific Ocean east into the Amazon jungle.

From around 1100 AD until the Spaniards arrived in 1533, Cusco was Rome, Mecca; every citizen tried to make a pilgrimage here before he died. And here, perhaps, begins my own.

A group of Indian women sit on the curbstone across the street, surrounded by large bundles. Each wears a white blouse and black fitted jacket, and their skirts fall in a pink-and-purple rainbow across the steps. Some hold a baby to their breasts while they spin yarn, chew coca leaves, and watch us from beneath their stiff white top hats. Tricia wonders if they will want money to take their picture. Kate hopes they won't. I watch a child leading a llama with tassels in its ears and wonder if the women on the corner find us three short, denim-and-khaki-clad females as exotic and interesting to them as they are to us.

It is our first day in Cusco. We arrived on an early flight from Lima, the fatigue of jet lag and an early departure alleviated by anticipation, as the plane banked and descended steeply between tawny terraced mountains, crossed a broad valley, and finally bounced along the tarmac. Chickens and dogs scurried to the sides, followed by children who waved as the plane nearly blew them off the runway.

The air was thin, cold, and invigorating. At the hotel, a young man checked us in and ordered coca tea to dispel the symptoms of soroche (altitude sickness), which include headache, nausea, sleeplessness, and irregular heartbeat. Kate informed us that it can strike young and old, fit and faint—anyone who takes lightly the sudden change in altitude from sea level to eleven thousand five hundred feet. Friends, books, and a notice at the hotel reception had all advised us to rest in our room the first day. Since our room was only on the second floor, I started up the stairs and arrived panting, heart pounding. Next time I took the elevator.

The room was cold. No sun streamed through the windows as it does on winter mornings in California. In this country, so close to the equator, the sun shines straight down. Often, it's warmer outside than in. The beds were small. The mattress, thin and hard, was covered with a white alpaca bedspread, soon to be littered with notepads, film, guidebooks, piles of clothing. We stashed our passports, tickets, money, cosmetics, and medicines on every shelf, nook, and ledge in bedroom and bathroom and stuffed bulging duffels under the bed. We would not need our sleeping bags, down parkas, and rain gear until we left for the horseback trip in a week. Wearily, we laid down amidst our possessions.

"Isn't it interesting how they inlaid all those little stones in cement—sort of a cave-like effect," Kate observed, looking up at the ceiling. "If there were an earthquake, the whole thing would bury us alive, and we wouldn't have to ride those horses."

Tricia groaned. "Do you always have to imagine the worst possible disaster? Let's get out of here."

Tired, yet unable to sleep, cold, hungry, and too curious to stay in our room, we surrendered to the lure of the street. Cameras around our necks, money concealed in belts, bras, and pockets, we descended to the lobby, ate a quick lunch, and headed out into the aptly named Calle del Sol.

Kate led the way to the Coricancha. As I climbed the steps to the temple, I could hear myself breathing. The temple was closed. *Thank God*, I thought, as I sat down on a large flat stone. Dizzy, head throbbing, I put my head down as if to search for pottery shards in the loose red dirt that was turning white and cloudy before my eyes. Tour groups were mingling about the entrance, and my companions had wandered off to inquire about opening hours. Never in my life had I passed out. This would be too embarrassing. *I can't be weak and helpless, not now, not here*, I thought. The dizziness subsided, but the headache didn't. I arose and walked slowly across the street, concentrating on the cobblestones, broken curbstone, holes, rocks, an open can of paint.

"Let's walk down this street to the Plaza de Armas," Kate said, looking at a map. "Are you all right?"

"Yes." I tried to look alert, attentive, engaged—but my mind was soaring across a sea of tile roofs and into the cauliflower clouds that hovered above the bare hills in the distance. I hoped this headache would go away. It was too bright, too hot in the sun, too cold in the shade of the walls of Calle Loreto.

Now, an hour later, I'm fully recovered (except for a slight headache), as we cross the plaza. The sounds, sights, and smells of Cusco assault us. Burros carrying bundles of straw, rugs, coca leaves, and other mysterious cargo trot noisily across cobbled streets, undeterred by honking buses, careening bicycles, zipping taxis. Unrecognizable animal parts sizzle over glowing coals at the *anticucho* stands, while the smoke carries the scent of garlic, red meat, and burning eucalyptus that mixes with the strong stench of urine trickling over the venerable stones.

The women of the plaza have moved across the street to a covered colonnade. They untie their bundles and arrange their wares on the stone floor. Hand-woven mantas (shawls) in vivid shades of red tell the stories of their weavers in intricate designs of birds, animals, and symbols of fertility and good harvests. Coca bags with long fringes are displayed in a row next to brass trinkets and ceramic pots. One woman nurses her baby while she unpacks a load of ponchos in alpaca earth tones. I find a large poncho in all the shades of llama hair: camel, brown, black, and cream. A fringe with little beads sewn on every strand encircles the hole in the middle, where one's head pokes through. Kate says it's too expensive and the beads will fall off. "I'll take it home and put it on the piano," I venture.

Tricia buys four hats with earflaps and buttons sewn all around and a huge carpet bag to transport all her purchases plus a hand-woven *cinta*, which she wraps around her waist, making a plain denim skirt seem suddenly festive. Using the Spanish she has learned from three winters living in Mexico, she smiles and cajoles the woman to give her a "*pequeña discuenta*."

Kate finds a black-and-gray alpaca sweater for eight dollars. She bargains vigorously, smiling and nodding her head in total agreement that, "*sí*, the quality is good, *sí*, it is *muy linda*, but no, it is *muy caro*." Bargaining is a sport for Kate, a contest and a game she plays with glee and determination. Smug when successful, she always pays less than we do. If Tricia thinks the price is too much, she doesn't buy it. I, on the other hand, make feeble attempts to barter, usually failing because the shopkeeper knows I'm a sucker. The indefinable line between dumb tourist who spends too much and the miserly slob who doesn't appreciate the native crafts will haunt me through this trip. I will return to buy my poncho when Kate isn't looking. Then I can pay too much without guilt.

We leave the women to bargain with new customers, as the streets around the Plaza de Armas become crowded with Peruvians gathering in groups on the now cold, shadowy streets. They talk softly in Quechua and look furtively at us.

"I think we had better go back to the hotel," Kate says.

"Do you hear a noise?" Tricia asks.

Beyond the walls of the Inca palaces, a sound like muffled thunder rumbles and swells until the throb and boom of drums resonates from the walls of the Calle Loreto and all the ancient stones of Cusco.

Helmeted policemen emerge from the side streets and encircle the plaza. They raise white batons in outstretched arms and form a barrier between the street that surrounds the plaza and a quiet but restless crowd, held back against the walls of the buildings.

"What's going on?" Tricia asks as we climb the stairs to the front of the cathedral.

"Must be a parade or something," I reply, thinking that if Osvaldo were here, he would insist on returning to the hotel. He warned me to avoid crowds—a fear born of life under dictatorships and revolutions.

WHEN I ASKED OSVALDO IF HE would come with me to Peru, he answered, "No, *mi esposa*. If I go to South America, I go to see my family in Argentina. Remember," he said, "I lived in a house with no heat, no running water. Every day, my brother and I carried water from a well three blocks away. We chopped wood, made a fire every day to heat the house and water for my mother to cook and wash our clothes. I was always cold. Do you think I'd pay to sleep outside on hard ground, no bathroom, no hot water—same thing I hated all those years growing up?" I had not thought of it as "the same thing," but then, I had not lived his life.

The solemn boom of drums increases in volume when fifty men with large red-and-white striped *bombas* (drums) slung over their left shoulders emerge from the Calle Loreto. Red patterned mantas, draped sling-like over their shoulders, contrast brightly on clean white shirts. While one arm beats the drum, the other holds a *zampoña* (pan-pipes) to waiting lips. Then, like wind whistling through rocks, the breathy notes of the *zampoñas* blow a universal sigh over the deep heavy *ba-boom* of the drums.

Another group enters the plaza, and then another. As they pass in front of the cathedral, musicians and dancers begin to dance a shuffling step-together-hop-step, bending and swaying to their own rhythm. Red, green, and yellow plumes on their hats dance in the breeze they create. Men with dark bony faces grin white teeth as they whirl in a frenzy of flying feathers. Men wearing *chullos* (knitted earflap hats with long tassels) carry willows that whip and whir through the air and crack on the pavement. Braids fly, as the women stomp and twirl their short black skirts and white petticoats in front of the whipping men.

A short dark man in a white shirt and black homespun pants sidles up to Tricia.

"*Son de Puno*," he tells her, pointing to the dancers. "*La cuña del folklorico.* (They are from Puno, the cradle of folklore.)" Tricia nods appreciatively.

We move back a few steps to give room to men wearing white knitted masks and suits of green fringe like moss, as they join the dancers with real leather whips. Kate asks me to ask Tricia's informer if anyone ever got hit by a whip. He tells me that once he was dancing in his village with a woman who had the whip, and if he didn't dance fast enough, or tried to get away, she whipped him. He laughs at the memory and crosses the street to join a group of women and children.

When the steady thud of the drums ceases and dancers and musicians disperse into crowded side streets to join friends and families from their villages, I wonder aloud if they will continue the party on the streets of Cusco tonight.

No one answers, as we realize we are being sucked into the crush of bodies moving away from the open plaza into a narrow side street. The crowd has become sullen and pushy, as two policemen hold us back to let a car get through.

"Hang onto your purse and let's get out of here," Kate says.

Chapter Two

LAS CONQUISTADORAS

▼▼▼▼▼▼▼▼▼▼▼▼▼▼▼

We follow Kate, still clutching her bag, into the hotel. Bright lights and a lobby full of tourists jolt me into my real world as a middle-aged female tourist. We wait while a group of Germans, packs slung over their shoulders, crowds the reception desk, eager for keys, a shower, a beer, and bed.

"Where have you been hiking?" Tricia asks a sunburned fräulein with Heidi-like pigtails.

"The Inca Trail," she answers. "Machu Picchu. Four days. Very good." She beams a triumphant smile.

The whir of a blender and the possibility of a pisco sour lures Kate to the bar in the alcove off the lobby, where the frothy concoction of Peruvian grape brandy blended with lime juice, sugar, and egg whites is being poured into glasses for a suntanned young man standing at the bar. Kate greets him, and by the time Tricia and I join them, Kate has learned that he is from Utah and has just made a first descent by canoe from high in the Andes down a river into the jungle of Bolivia. He tells us of encounters with snakes, mosquitoes, and unexplored rapids. I envy his youth and his stamina, and I applaud the fact that he had the guts and the imagination to do this.

The heartrending lament of a *huayno* weeps on the strings of an Andean harp as we climb the stairs to our room. Exhausted, yet energized, I welcome the disarray of familiar objects festooned about our room.

"How do you feel?" Kate asks, opening her medicine bag on the bed. "Does anyone have *soroche*?"

Tricia looks at her face in the bathroom mirror. Pink cheeks, freckles, slightly mussed hair. "I'm fine," she answers. "Either the pills you gave me are working, or we just aren't going to get it."

"What pills?" I wonder, fearing I have been left out of some important medical decision.

"Diamox for altitude sickness," Kate says. "You have to take it ahead of time. It makes you feel tingly."

"So that's why I thought my fingers were going to sleep," Tricia says.

So that's why I nearly passed out today, I think.

"The doctors at the office gave it to me," Kate informs us.

"Is memory affected by altitude?" I wonder. "I just had my wallet, and now I can't find it." Tricia hands it to me from the bedside table. "Now I can't remember what I was going to put in it." Everything seems to be floating about the room and changing positions without my control. I can't remember where I put anything.

"What are you looking for?" Tricia asks.

"I can't remember which pocket I put my credit cards in. I guess I don't need them. Where are my glasses?"

"They're on the windowsill." Kate hands them to me.

"Where's the key?" Tricia glances around the cluttered surfaces of the room.

The phone rings. "Where is it?"

"In the waste basket."

"Hola, gringas," Bill says, calling us from the lobby. "When did you get here? How was the flight? Are you hungry?"

We agree to meet for dinner in fifteen minutes.

BILL'S HUG IS FIRM AND SINCERE. He introduces us to Brad and his wife, Patti, who will join us on the trip tomorrow to the Urubamba Valley and on the horseback trip. Dressed in jeans and sweatshirts, they have a rumpled, well-traveled appearance. We learn later that the names and happy faces on their T-shirts belong to grandchildren at home in Los Angeles.

Marilyn and Philippe, already seated at our table, will assist Bill on our trip and work with him as guides on future trips. Marilyn came to South America as a guide for a New York travel agency and has "done" the Inca Trail eleven times. Philippe, Belgian by birth, was a naturalist and guide in the Galápagos for fifteen years. Recently married, they live in Ecuador.

Brad and Patti have just traveled from La Paz, Bolivia, across Lake Titicaca and the Altiplano to Cusco. Since Kate, Tricia, and I plan to do the same in reverse, we are curious about their experiences, and they are eager to share them.

Patti begins, "On our last night in La Paz, our guide took us to a local 'dive' where we joined his buddies playing guitars, charangos, pipes, flutes—you name it. We banged on tables, sang, whistled, drank some rot-gut alcohol, chewed coca leaves, and Carlos, our guide, was so drunk, we had to carry him back to our hotel."

Brad, chuckling at the memory of that night, tells his bathroom story: "There was a curtain in a corner of the room that I guessed was the bathroom. It had no drain—so I looked at Carlos, wondering where to aim. You should have seen the grin when he let loose at random. We made patterns on the walls together."

"When you go from Bolivia to Peru by bus," Patti explains, "the road follows the shore of Lake Titicaca until you get to the straits of Taquini, where the bus and all your belongings go on a ferry, and you go with the passengers in a launch."

"We'll be going from Peru to Bolivia," Kate says.

"Yes, you will take the bus from Puno. Well, the launch wasn't tied," Patti continues, "and the captain couldn't have been over thirteen. With about thirty of us crammed on board, he poled away from the dock, while the water rose to about knee deep. By the time we reached the middle, everyone was screaming, babies wailing, and desperate Indian women with heavy wet petticoats were shoving and pushing in an effort to scramble onto higher seats on the upper deck. I'm sure we were the only ones who knew how to swim."

"When we reached the other side," Brad adds, "I was sure someone would be trampled. One man fell in. I was the last to leap ashore just as the boat sank." Brad and Patti share triumphant grins.

Bill, Marilyn, and Philippe laugh their approval, as a round of pisco sours is delivered to the table. Enjoying this tale of potential adventure, I ask about the bus trip to Puno on the Peruvian shore of Lake Titicaca.

"That part was okay," Patti replies, "but generally, buses are unreliable, filthy, and dangerous. When we got to Puno, we decided to take a side trip by bus to Arequipa—before taking the train to Cusco. We drove around town for hours, looking for passengers to fill it up. Forget schedules."

Dinner arrives, and our attention and forks turn to a tasty stir-fry of rice, fried potatoes, beef strips, onions, and peas. *Saltado* will become a staple in Peru.

We return to our room and try to focus on packing for a raft trip down the Urubamba River, followed by two days (and two markets!) in the Urubamba Valley. We putter, rummage, and mumble as we assemble:

- knapsack for tomorrow (camera, first aid, bathing suit, shoes, sunscreen, hat)
- bag for two nights—warm clothes?
- bag to leave at the hotel (nice clothes, skirts, new purchases)
- saddle bag with camping and riding gear
- passports and plane tickets to be left at the front desk

Finally, at almost midnight, I lie back with my head on a pillow as hard as an Inca stone and close my eyes on a day that began at five in the morning in Lima.

THREE DAYS AGO, WE LANDED in Lima at midnight. A taxi whisked us down deserted streets, around potholes, and past shuttered stores.

"*Donde esta la gente?* (Where are the people?)" I asked.

"*Toque de queda.* (A curfew)," the driver replied.

"*Por qué?*"

"*Pués hay ladrones* (thieves)," he told me—terrorists perhaps. The curfew begins at one in the morning. After that, you must have a permit from the police to be on the street. *Perhaps all the grim warnings from friends and families were true*, I thought.

My husband had warned me, "Be careful."

"Why?"

"Because women don't travel alone in South America."

"Why?"

"Because they are easy prey, especially Americans."

"But I am a fifty-year-old woman. They'll respect me."

"In Peru, there are kidnappers, bandits—people who don't like Americans."

"I'll be with a group, with Kate and Tricia."

"I know you, *mi esposa*. You will go off exploring on your own and get into trouble. I'll feel better if Kate is with you."

Sensible, sturdy, dependable Kate—my safety would be insured by her competent company.

Marble floors, burnished wood panels, and a concierge dressed like a kindly undertaker reassured us that the Hotel Bolivar was safe. When a military coup took over the government in 1968, my parents had to stay inside the hotel for three days, while demonstrations took place on the plaza outside. We collected our keys and free drink tickets. The bar was closed, but three pisco sours would be delivered to our room. They arrived minutes later on a silver tray.

"I like this old hotel," Tricia said.

The next morning, we decided to change money across the street. Friends, spouses, savvy travelers—all had warned us of bag snatchers and pack rippers. I had a small white purse strapped to my bra. Kate and Tricia had sewn pockets to the inside of their skirts, forcing them to either stick their hands into their waistbands or reach up and under their skirts, exposing pink gringo thighs. Osvaldo assured us that pickpockets would be waiting for us outside our hotels. Our only salvation might be that they weren't as expert as the ones in Argentina.

I entered a small *Casa de Cambio,* heeding Kate's warning to look cool and nonchalant. I read the signs about the exchange rate, then slid a hundred-dollar bill under the window. Faster than eyes could count, the clerk dealt out four hundred and seventy thousand soles in five teetering stacks of about twenty bills. It must have looked like a fortune to the people standing in line behind me.

"Gracias," I said, abandoning the route up under my sweater, down my shirt, and into a much too-small purse. As I stuffed the worn and wrinkled soles into my pocket, an Indian woman approached me from behind and tapped me firmly on the elbow.

"Señora . . ."

Here it comes—the classic diversion, then the hit, I thought.

She handed me a US fifty-dollar bill I had dropped on the floor. I thanked her and joined my friends on the street, grateful not only for the fifty dollars, but mostly for my restored faith. My instincts told me to trust these gentle people, while Kate and Tricia rolled their eyes in wonder how anyone could be so gullible. Somewhere there is a zone between caution and paranoia.

The crowded, chaotic, and colorless city closed in around us as we joined the parade of shoppers, street vendors, beggars, and businessmen on a pedestrian street that led to the Plaza de Armas.

WHEN PIZARRO PLANNED THIS CITY in 1535, he laid it out in a grid pattern, where sixty Spanish families lived on seventeen lots. Peru was the only Andean nation with a seaport, and twice a year, the Spanish fleet sailed into port bringing men, horses, and goods from Spain to be distributed in the vice royalty of Peru and, later, to Ecuador, Bolivia, Chile, and Argentina.

In 1851, the first railway in South America linked the port of Callao to Lima (ten miles inland) and continued up into the silver and tin mines of the Andes. Lima was the largest city in the Americas, maintaining a robust economy well into the eighteenth century. A devastating earthquake in 1746, followed by the closing of the mines in Bolivia plus the establishment by the Spanish of a viceroyalty and a port on the Atlantic (Buenos Aires) slowed the economy—but not the population. It catapulted from six hundred thousand in 1940 to two million in 1961 to more than six million today. One third live in shantytowns that surround the city.

Kate, guidebook in hand, identified important buildings: the cathedral, the Presidential Palace, the former Viceroy's Palace (originally built on the site of Pizarro's house), the Archbishop's Palace, and the Cabildo. Intricately carved wooden balconies, loosely attached to buildings and probably too dangerous to step out on, seemed to me typically Peruvian—an impractical and romantic statement on the walls of colonial tradition.

After lunch, we took a cab to the residential area of Miraflores. I had just read *Aunt Julia and the Scriptwriter*, and could imagine Varquitos and Tia Julia sipping coffee in any of the sidewalk cafés. Mario Vargas Llosa, Peruvian author and recipient of the 2010 Nobel Prize for literature, had captured the endearing characteristics of a neighborhood both cosmopolitan and innocent—a place that doesn't take itself too seriously. Well-cared-for homes in a variety of sizes, colors, and styles were interspersed with foreign consulates, modern glass hotels, apartment houses, and garden restaurants. Boutiques and little shaded walkways revealed shopping arcades with native hand-crafts and antiques. Some hotels had huge flowering trees enclosed in quiet gardens.

Ice cream vendors, pushing their carts down empty streets, broke the silence with a shrill whistle. We stopped to admire the fruit in one of the many carts parked on street corners. The owners pull them into place in the early morning hours, staying there until dark.

Tricia bought a *grenadilla* (passion fruit) and sucked on the slimy seeds as we inspected the contents of the cart. The papayas were as big as footballs, the avocados almost as large.

"Guavas are higher in vitamin C than oranges," Kate informed us.

"What are those?" Tricia asked in Spanish, pointing to a large green fruit.

"Chirimoyas," the cart-tender replied, awakening a sleeping baby wrapped in a blanket between the chirimoyas and papayas.

We were curious to taste this unknown fruit, green like an artichoke and shaped like a pineapple without a stem, but we didn't know how to approach it. Did you peel it?

At dinner that night, in a restaurant at the end of a pier, we ordered chirimoya sundaes for dessert. It had the consistency of custard and tasted like a cross between banana, coconut, pear, and everything tropical. No wonder the Incas prized it, even without hot fudge sauce, chewy chunks of meringue, and vanilla ice cream!

After dinner, Tricia and I watched the sun set on the Pacific while Kate bribed two children to find a taxi. They returned with a young man wearing an undershirt and torn jeans. As he careened around pot-holes, stray animals, and slower vehicles, we gripped the torn plastic seat covers. He laughed and sang while his radio blared rock music. At every intersection, whether the light was red or green, he put his hand to the horn and his foot on the gas. Tricia put her face in her hands. Kate looked accusingly at me.

Suddenly, the car screeched and skidded sideways to a stop at a green light. "Why is he stopping when the light's green?" Kate asked, and I repeated the question in Spanish.

"*Porque viene otro de aquel lado.* (Because another car was going through the red light.)"

"This country is very fucked up," Kate said, and I could tell she was scared.

He charged us double, and Kate complained that he had quoted us a different price when he picked us up. When I questioned him, he explained that it was daytime rates until nine. It was nine fifteen, he said, and he got us here twice as fast, so we should pay more.

A pisco sour in the bar of the open-air balcony would calm shattered nerves. Warm air rose from the street below, carrying with it the pleasant murmur of Spanish voices.

Kate scrutinized the clientele. "Look at those three couples." She nodded in the direction of a group of Americans. "Too well-dressed to be tourists, too loud to be locals—maybe businessmen, lawyers, probably, with their wives."

"No," Tricia replied, "diplomats—international types . . ."

"And we are three middle-aged housewives on a tour without our husbands," Kate said, "nondescript women in sensible shoes— products of the fifties—dependable but dull."

Another round of piscos, and we were convinced we were three brilliant, sensitive, fearless friends. We would conquer Peru in our unique way. The more pisco we drank, the better we liked ourselves.

Chapter Three

URUBAMBA

*The Sacred Valley
of the Incas*

▼▼▼▼▼▼▼▼▼▼▼▼▼▼

At eight o'clock the next morning, Tricia, Kate, and I join the other members of our group in the hotel lobby. Packs on backs, overnight bags slung over shoulders, we are eager and slightly giddy with altitude and anticipation of our first adventure, a float down the Urubamba River. An hour passes while we wait for our river guide. Marilyn goes out to the street to look for the van.

Bill has gone to arrange for food and equipment for the horseback trip, so we can't complain to him. We speculate about the river—will there be Indian villages? Wildlife? Will it be cold? How long? Pat and Brad tell us more travel tales and bad bathroom stories. Marilyn returns. Philippe calls the local tour office that arranged our trip. Where are they? On their way . . . they left an hour ago.

Marilyn tells us about hiking the Inca Trail and her wedding in Ecuador. Philippe goes outside to look for the van. Another hour passes.

Suddenly, the hotel door opens, and a tall, dark-skinned man with messy, thick, black hair strides into the lobby. "My name is

George, or you can call me Jorge," he says in unaccented English. "I overslept."

He looks Peruvian, sounds American. We pile into a white van and drive four blocks through the now crowded back streets of Cusco, then stop at a garage to pick up ropes, paddles, and life preservers. We wait inside the van while Philippe helps George load it on the roof and tie it down with the ropes.

"Why didn't he do this yesterday," Kate wonders.

"Or at least before he picked us up," Pat adds.

We stop again to buy gas, then soft drinks. None of us has any idea where we are going or how long it will take. The "early morning departure" has become the "whenever ready departure."

"I don't see why they never do anything when they say they will," Pat remarks, with an "I-told-you-so" nod of her head.

WE WIND OUR WAY UP AND OUT of Cusco to a high plain overlooking the Urubamba Valley, where George pulls off the road and stops to let us get out and take pictures.

"Machu Picchu is beyond those mountains," he says.

Basking in the sun between Cusco and Machu Picchu, the "Sacred Valley of the Incas" is protected on either side by two mountain ranges: the Urubamba to the northeast, and the Vilcabamba to the west. Both ranges have nineteen-thousand-foot peaks with glaciers that seem to float above the clouds, eternally frozen far above the fields, terraces, and villages that have been cultivated and inhabited for centuries by the Incas, their descendants, the conquering Spaniards, and present-day campesinos.

A multihued poncho of gold, green, russet, and ochre—the colors of the earth and surrounding hills—wraps us in its undulating folds, as we switchback down to the valley floor. Pale gray-green clouds of eucalyptus groves look foreign and unnatural—like palm

Above the Urubamba Valley

trees growing in the snow. Brad confirms what we suspected, that they were planted by the conquering Spaniards.

Along the road, piles of clay tiles lie drying in the sun. George stops so we can watch a man and a woman making tiles for their roof. The man's sun-bronzed muscles strain under the weight of a heavy load of mud. His smile is as bright as his white shirt. We watch him plop the soft red clay on a semicircular mold, spread it out with a roller, and pat and shape it with expert hands. His wife carries the newly shaped tile in its mold to a place where it will dry. Slipping the mold out from underneath, she returns for the next one. Their motions are economical, energetic, and carefree. Not bothered by our curiosity or picture taking, they wave a friendly greeting.

We travel in silence for twenty minutes before George turns off the main route onto a dirt road that leads down to our "put-in" spot on the river. "About two more miles," he says. Stones fly and clouds of dust envelop us as he tries to make up the time he lost oversleeping.

The steep, bumpy road drops straight down to the river's edge, where we skid to a stop in the sand. The slate-blue water of the Urubamba River flows peacefully before us, looking cool and indifferent to our arrival.

George's helpers, Tony and Manolo, have been waiting for us all morning. They help us pull the deflated rafts off the top of the van. George produces a broken pump. While he tries to fix it, we assist Tony and Manolo in inflating the rafts with a hand pump.

An hour later, we are ready to float to an unknown destination. Most of the group is eager to grab an oar and do their own navigating in Manolo's raft. The cold water, dark clouds, light rain, a stomachache, and the sight of my white, goose-pimpled legs shivering in baggy shorts has diminished my enthusiasm, so I opt to join Tricia in a smaller raft, where we can sit idly and look up at the steep terraces on either side of us while Tony rows, keeping the raft straight in the placid river. Fair-skinned, lean, and wiry, he looks more European than Peruvian. An experienced kayaker and river guide, he knows most of the rivers in Peru and Bolivia.

"Why don't more Americans come to Peru?" he asks in Spanish. "You have so many active young people; why don't they come here?"

"Unfortunately," I begin, "many Americans don't know much about Peru or South America."

"Most kids out of college want to see Europe before anything else," Tricia says. "Probably because their parents are paying for it."

"Most of the tourists who come here for adventure travel are older women," Tony says, while paddling deftly through a small eddy. "Perhaps younger ones don't like adventure."

"Oh, I'm sure they do," I say, wondering if this present activity would be considered "adventure travel." I think about the adults who told me Peru was dirty and dangerous and asked how my husband could let me go there alone (as if *alone* meant *without him*).

"Perhaps we Americans think we should see the countries whose culture and history we share," Tricia says. "We study Europe, and our parents tell us about the great museums and cities."

"Lots of Europeans come to Peru," Tony says. "They don't come on tours like Americans." He looks puzzled but resigned to the mistaken priorities of the North American youth.

"Peru has a reputation for being dangerous," Tricia says. "Coming here requires planning, and it's hard to know how to travel here without a guide or a tour."

"For some people, that's the best part, the challenge, the adventure, going where you don't know everything ahead of time," I say, thinking aloud. "Actually, I wish I had taken trips like this when I was younger. Experiencing a culture I knew nothing about is an adventure in itself."

"That's true," Tricia says. "I never would have had the nerve to come here when I was younger. My parents wouldn't have allowed me!" she says, sitting up and rocking the raft.

"I think mine would have—if it had ever occurred to me in the first place," I reply.

We approach the first rapid. George watches from a cliff above us, his camera ready. Manolo, perched on the back of the other raft, shouts, "*Izquierda!* (Left)," then "*Derecha!* (Right.)" Brad, Pat, Kate, Philippe, and Marilyn paddle hard, keeping their craft straight. We watch them bounce over some underwater rocks when suddenly Manolo is flung from his perch into the river. Gleeful shrieks echo through the canyon, and Tony smiles for the first time today.

I'm glad when, at last, we pull the rafts ashore on a sandy beach where George is waiting with lunch. Verbally and physically bilingual, he instructs us in English how to rinse, dry, and deflate the rafts, then speaks in Spanish to his helpers with the mannerisms and expressions of a Peruvian, including the regional intonation of Quechua.

With dripping rafts and oars loaded atop the van, we roar down the paved road to Pisac. Children, goats, dogs, and stout women with bundles on their backs flee from our path. I sink down into the seat feeling sharp stomach pains, wondering what I'll do if suddenly I need a bathroom. George swerves around loose animals and wandering *campesinos*. Bouncing in and out of potholes, we speed along a stretch of dirt road. The car fills with dust before we can get the windows up.

Pat asks Brad to ask George to slow down. She also asks him to ask about available bathrooms in Pisac, and I await the answer with a surge of optimism.

"There are no bathrooms in Pisac," he says, turning around to the back seat, while the car hurtles onward. "Once you leave your hotel, you won't find a bathroom anywhere in Peru," he adds cheerily.

"Or at least none you might want to enter," Brad adds.

We slow down at a bridge that spans the Urubamba, stopping when armed guards in camouflage suits approach the van. George greets them respectfully, shows them some papers, and is asked to get out of the car and come into the small guard station, leaving us alone.

"What do you suppose this is about?" Tricia asks.

"Probably want him to pay a bribe," Brad says.

"Or maybe kill him and kidnap us for ransom," Kate suggests.

"Jesus, Kate, why do you always imagine the worst possible scenario?" Tricia says. George returns, stuffing some bills into his pocket.

"I knew it," says Pat. "George, did you pay a bribe to get us into Pisac?"

"No," he replies. "See, they gave me a receipt." He holds up a small piece of paper. "Pisac has been declared a national landmark, so they collect taxes, just like your national parks in the States."

"Then they must have bathrooms," Brad adds hopefully.

"I will ask in a restaurant," George promises as he parks the van in front of a bar advertising "Inca Cola." We are invited to the back of the building, where a door opens to a black hole.

Meanwhile, George is inquiring where we can buy *trago*. He wants us to try the local brandy, which is made of raw cane alcohol. We find a store that has some in a tin gas can. The wizened but amiable proprietor pours a portion of a liquid resembling kerosene into George's outstretched tin cup, fills a presumably washed bottle, and corks it with the tip of a corn cob.

George offers Kate the first taste. She takes a timid sip, grimaces, and asks, "Why do they call this rotgut *trago*?"

"Must be because *trago* means sip," I reply.

"Well that's definitely the best way to drink it," Kate replies.

On the way back to the car, I ask George in Spanish why the guards wear camouflage gear and carry guns. "A guard was shot there two days ago," he replies.

"Why? Bandits?"

"Don't know," he answers. "Could have been bandits, but they don't usually have guns. Could have been terrorists trying to get into town and cause trouble."

"Here?" I look around at the peaceful square, where the blossoms of pisonay trees have laid a lavender carpet over the stench of urine, dog shit, and the remains of rotting fruits.

"*Quien sabe*," he replies with a shrug.

Early evening we arrive at the *Residencia Naranjachoya* (house with an orange tree) near the town of Urubamba. A former hacienda, its walls are surrounded by orchards and cultivated fields. Through an iron gate, I find an empty swimming pool. Paths wander off through a neglected garden, and a parrot named Pepe observes our arrival from a flowering pisonay tree. One building consists of bedrooms surrounding a courtyard in the middle of which is the orange tree. Another building houses a large dining room and a bar with a fireplace where a fire has just been lit.

Wet sneakers and hiking boots steam on the hearth, while rafters, guides, and passengers relax in soft leather chairs and enjoy beer and Inca Colas. Manolo and Tony recount a seven-day raft trip in Peru and Bolivia on the Tambopata River, where the jungle is rich with wildlife, and there is no way out until the end.

A newspaper from Cusco lies open on the bar. Kate is trying to read beneath the headline, "*Sendero Luminoso*."

She gives it to George, "What's this?"

"The Shining Path," he answers. "They are terrorists, and they have declared war on us."

"On us?" she asks.

"Well, actually on Peru," he answers.

"Are they the terrorists that kill people in the villages if they don't join the cause?" she asks, and I am impressed at Kate's knowledge. Tricia joins them and reads the article in Spanish.

"They are Maoists," she comments. "Where is Ayacucho?"

"It's north of here," George answers. "That's where they're centered, but it seems they've taken over other villages, moving south through the foothills." Brad joins us at the bar. "Did you hear about them blowing up the power station and cutting off the electricity in Lima?" he asks.

"Yes," George answers. "So far the government hasn't acknowledged them. That ought to wake 'em up."

I dash across the patio to our room. After a megadose of Pepto Bismol, I take a long, hot shower. Later, when I hear woeful tales of no hot water, I don't apologize. I'm surprised at my complete lack of guilt and feeling of entitlement, due to my condition.

This is my first lesson in the art of survival, as we travel by bus, horse, and foot over the Andes: that blind luck beats the best laid plans, preparations, and schemes—that if you get the only hot shower, the warmest spot in the truck, the only level tent site, or the last of the pisco, *take it*! Accept it as a gift of fate. You may be sorry later.

I sit next to George at dinner that night, and when I ask him about Peruvian writers, he tells me, "Mario Vargas Llosa is a snob."

"But I loved *Aunt Julia and the Scriptwriter*. The characters seem so uniquely Peruvian," I say.

"Well, I know him. We went to the same school in Lima. Did you know he's a communist?" George adds, pouring us both another glass of wine.

"Who do you think is the greatest Peruvian writer?" I ask.

"Jose Maria Arguedas, without a doubt. Have you heard of him?" he asks.

"No," I reply. George writes the name on a paper napkin, and when I return to California and order his books, I find this to be true.

BORN IN 1911, ARGUEDAS GREW UP in the rural community of Andahuaylas in the house of his stepmother, who, by his own account, "owned half the town; she had many indigenous servants, and with it, the traditional contempt for and lack of awareness of what an Indian was."

Arguedas's mother, a mestizo (Spanish and Quechua) woman, died when he was two years old, leaving him home with his stepmother and her children, whom he did not like. He found love and solace in the kitchen with the servants, where he ate, slept, and lived, except for the occasions when his father would visit, and he would dress up and eat in the dining room with his parents and three stepsiblings.

In the introduction to *Deep Rivers*, Arguedas's third novel, published in 1958, anthropology professor and expert on Inca culture John Murra quotes Arguedas from remarks the writer made at a gathering of fiction writers in June 1965, in Arequipa.

> *"My bed was a wooden trough of the kind used to knead bread. Resting on some sheepskins and covered with a rather dirty but very sheltering blanket, I spent the nights talking and living so well that if my stepmother had known it she would have removed me to her side . . .*
>
> *"The Indians, particularly their women, saw me as one of them, with the difference that being white, I needed even more comforting than they did, and this they gave me in full. But consolation must contain within it both sadness and power; as those tormented comforted those who suffered even more, two things were sadly driven into my nature from the time I learned to speak: 1) the tenderness and limitless love of the Indians, the love they feel for each other and for nature, the highlands, rivers, and birds; (2) the hatred they felt for those*

who, almost as if unaware and seeming to follow an order on high, made them suffer. My childhood went by, singed between fire and love."

Thus began a lifetime of torment. Torn between two worlds— that of the Indians who brought him up and taught him about love, binding him inexorably to the land they were a part of, and that of the white Spaniards, whose world he was born to and would have to live in. Frustrated and angry with the attitudes of his own race and clearly identifying with the race he didn't belong to, he could not escape the confrontations of these two hostile cultures. Arguedas personifies the racial struggle which continues to shape the history of Peru. He committed suicide in 1969.

DURING DINNER, 1 ASK GEORGE about his family and what it's like living in Cusco. "I love Cusco," he says. "Close to nature and surrounded by good friends. I grew up and went to school in Lima. I hate Lima."

"Why? Are your parents still there?"

"Yes, my father works in the American Embassy. My mother is Peruvian—mestizo."

I look at him inquiringly, "Just like Arguedas?"

"Yes. In Lima, the upper-class white Spanish community doesn't accept people with Indian blood. My American father could never understand that, and I guess I didn't, either—just kind of accepted it, you know."

"That must have been difficult."

"The worst part was getting beaten up by the mestizo kids who hated my guts for being Anglo."

"I didn't know there was so much racism in Peru," I remark. "In Argentina there are no Indians."

"Yeah, because they killed them all or put them in reservations just like you guys did." He looks at me somewhat accusingly, and I feel ashamed, apologetic, but say nothing.

We eat fresh trout and tasty potatoes in silence, and I recall an incident that occurred with two Chilean sisters I knew in San Francisco. They had both finished studying in Santiago and were traveling around the world.

When I told them I was engaged to an Argentine, they warned, "You must be careful that he doesn't have Indian blood."

"Why?" I asked.

"If he lives in the Andes (which he did), he might be part Indian. Is his skin dark?"

"No, not really."

"Well, if he is dark and has dark spots on his lower back, he may have Indian blood."

I wanted to laugh, make a joke, but I realized this was serious to them, so I promised to look for the spots. As it turned out, not only does *he* have the dreaded spots, so do all three of my children.

With new insight into that long-ago conversation, I turn to George.

"Is it better living in Cusco? It seems almost everyone around here is Indian or mestizo."

"No." He wraps his fork and knife neatly in a napkin. "My wife is French, but our kids are mestizo, just like me. One is blond. The rest are dark. They get beat up and teased just like I did, but I like Cusco better because I love the outdoors."

Two of my children are dark like their father, and the youngest is blond. People used to ask if he was adopted.

The electricity goes off at ten at night, and dessert is served by candlelight.

"Do you think the Senderos blew up the electrical plant?" Kate asks.

"No, the electricity always goes off here at ten," George says with a laugh.

He and Kate discuss terrorism in the flickering shadows. "They've actually done a hell of a lot of damage," he admits. "Blown up bridges, electrical plants, water supplies, but nothing around here."

"Have they killed any foreigners?" Kate asks.

"Not that I know of. Seems they hate Russian communists as much as American capitalists. They hate everyone. Last week they put a bomb in a Russian fishing boat."

"That newspaper said there are certain places tourists shouldn't go," Kate says.

"Oh yeah, that's up north and in the jungle," George replies. "They don't have police protection, and they've killed the mayors in some of those small villages. You wouldn't want to go there anyway." He goes to get a beer.

During the night, I am awakened by the sound of the curtains being pulled aside. Kate is at the window and beckons me to join her. Four *campesinos* are walking soundlessly in single file across a moonlit field. They stop once and look back toward a farmhouse, then continue.

"What do you think they're doing?" she asks.

"Coming home from a party," I reply.

"At this hour? Farm workers out this late? They're terrorists," she declares.

"Maybe they're coming home from a movie," Tricia mumbles from under her covers.

"They're not interested in us," I state with some authority. "If they're terrorists, they're out recruiting followers from the village." I return to bed. The sheets are warm and comforting, another Inca stone pillow. The bathroom is nearby. *No problemas*.

Chapter Four

MARKETS AND
MYSTERIES

Rocks, Rivers,

Terraces, Tombs

▼▼▼▼▼▼▼▼▼▼▼▼▼▼▼

George has returned to Cusco, and a new driver, Raul, arrives promptly at nine the next morning in a blue van with "Southern Cross Adventures" printed on its door. Soft Brillo-pad curls stray from beneath a plaid cap, and full lips open into a smile that turns down at the corners, revealing perfect white teeth. He looks directly into my eyes and asks how I learned to speak Spanish.

When I tell him my husband is Argentine, he winks, imitating an Argentine accent, and says, "*Che, vos sos casada. Que pena, che. Pero no soy selosa.* (Hey, you're married. Too bad. But I'm not jealous.)"

Again, we drive down the valley, on our way to the markets at Chinchero and Pisac. When we turn off the main road, I catch a glimpse of two burros, tethered to a pole, walking around in slow circles.

Marilyn, sitting in the front seat, anticipates my question. "They're threshing wheat—just like the Incas did it."

We climb steep switchbacks to a high plateau. Adobe farm-houses, the same rich brown as the recently plowed earth around them, pass in a blur of fields and farmyards. Sparkling diamond peaks rise in the distance, contrasting sharply with the warm, productive earth.

Raul parks on a level lot, and I shoulder my pack, eager to be off and up the steep rocky path to the market. I can't keep up with Marilyn or Philippe. Heart pounding, I pause at the top of the stairway.

"We are at twelve thousand four hundred feet," Patti announces, guidebook in hand.

Raul leads us through a stone archway to the market. Spread on the grass, close in the shade of an Inca wall, pyramids of fruit, vegetables, onions, coca leaves, plants, herbs, and grasses await the local trade. For the tourists, *chicha* cups, gourds, and clay pots (some broken, some whole) stand in orderly rows next to stacks of alpaca sweaters, rubber sandals, ponchos, mantas, hats, and woven belts. The bright pinks, reds, blues, and yellows of acrylic yarn look garish next to the softer hues of vegetable-dyed alpaca, and I am sorry that either the tourist trade or some aberration of taste has caused modern weavers to prefer the synthetic over pure alpaca.

Tupos (antique silver pins) in the form of a bird or a spoon lie in rows on blue plastic sheets. *Tupos* are the old-fashioned way to fasten a poncho together across the chest. The modern way, I have noticed, is with a safety pin.

Burros, laden with burlap sacks of potatoes and coca leaves, wander through the market. A young mother spreads her hand-woven *lliclla*, a large shawl, on the grass and puts her baby, some bananas, a tin cup, and some pieces of cloth on top. Then she folds it like an envelope, swings the whole thing up onto her back, and ties it in front. Amazingly, the baby and the bananas don't go flying across the square into a pile of coca leaves.

All about me, the centuries-old activity of buying, selling, bartering, bribing, and begging is carried on in a melodic chant of Quechua and Spanish.

"*Comprame, comprame algo, señora. Señora . . . por favor . . . muy barato . . . alpaca pura.* (Buy something from me, please, madam, very cheap, pure alpaca)," they implore, as I walk along the aisles admiring the intricate patterns of birds, plants, and geometric designs—hundreds of hand-woven mantas, ponchos, and belts, no two alike. I wonder whether to buy a poncho for the horseback trip, or a manta, a rug, a pot to take home, earrings for my daughter?

The women wear full skirts with many petticoats, white blouses, and embroidered vests, some very old and faded, probably handed down through the family. A little felt-covered disc balances on their heads, and an intricate mass of braids, mysteriously tied in tangled loops, streams over their shoulders.

I long for a Chinchero hat. On close examination, I discover it is not made of cardboard, as I suspected, but of tightly woven straw with a slight indentation for the head. All the women in the market wear these hats. They lean forward to arrange their wares, careful not to wake babies sleeping or nursing in their laps. They turn sideways to gossip and chat with neighbors. They look up into the sun with brown squinting eyes to address a customer. Why don't their hats fall off?

Tricia and Kate are on a manta mission, Patti and Brad taking photos.

I cross the market to inspect a massive Inca wall with ten large (for an Inca) man-sized niches. Leaving the hum of rural commerce in the market below, I climb a stairway to the upper square, where a large colonial church, crumbling but dominating, stands with its doors open. The sounds of devout recitations in Quechua slip through the doors and dissolve in the sun-soaked plaza. A group of men lean against the wall in the shade of the

bell tower, chewing coca leaves and staring at a pile of rocks supporting a cross in the middle of the square, where three women
have stopped to rest their heavy loads. Raul is sitting on a bench
watching a group of boys play a loosely defined game of soccer.
He sees me and walks over.

"*Que haces, aqui, mujer linda?* (What are you doing here, pretty
woman?)"

Flustered, flattered, surprised, I answer, "*Nada*. Just looking
around . . ."

"Come here, I will show you something," he says in Spanish.

We walk to the left of the church and down a stone staircase.

"These were the houses of the Incas," he tells me, pointing
to what must have been the foundations. "The stones are small
because they carried them up from the valley below."

We step outside of the wall that surrounds the town and follow
a path to the edge of a hillside with an unexpected panorama
of rolling hills rising to steep mountain slopes. Terraces upon
terraces climb every mountainside in view, and in the distance, the
resolute white wall of the Cordillera Villcabamba rises above it
all, separating the valley below from what I imagine to be miles of
steamy unexplored jungle, unnavigable rivers, undiscovered Inca
palaces, unknown tombs, and impassable trails that disappear into
the Amazon watershed.

Raul takes my hand and leads me over rough terrain to a large
rock outcrop carved and sculpted into stairs, canals, seats, and perhaps tombs.

"Go, look," he says, pointing to a narrow passageway.

I squeeze between two piano-size boulders, grateful that I don't
get stuck. Raul follows. In front of me, a staircase climbs up from
our dark cave to the rocks above. Raul slides his dark smooth hands
across the granite to find the first of many handholds, carved at just
the right intervals to facilitate our climb to the top. We emerge on a

rocky outcrop that overlooks a great sweep of terraced slopes rising from a narrow valley.

"*Vení aquí* (come here)," he says, indicating a carved stone seat. He tells me it was the Inca's throne. We sit together like king and queen surveying our kingdom. Raul points out a canal that still carries water from a spring below us to terraces far off on another hillside.

"I always come here when I come to Chinchero," he tells me in Spanish.

"I'm glad you brought me. I never would have known or seen all those mountains . . . terraces . . . walls. The market is amazing, but this is even more so . . . in a different way."

"Who lived here? What was this?" I wonder aloud.

Raul gazes across the rolling altiplano to distant snow-capped peaks. "We call this area the Pampa Anta, because it is high and flat," he says. "Before the Spaniards came and tore it down, Chinchero was an important city. It probably was the home of Topa Inca, Pachacuti's son."

I try to imagine Pachacuti, founder and emperor of the Incas, builder of Cusco, and conqueror of the Chancas and later the Aymara, sitting here and pointing out to his son where to build terraces and what crops to plant where.

"You can walk from here down an old Inca road to the Urubamba River in the valley."

That sounds like a great idea, something I would do, if my friends and the bus weren't in the opposite direction.

With his deep-set eyes, flat nose, high cheekbones, and smooth skin, Raul is probably more Indian than George. His indisputable ethnicity allows him the privilege of pride and identity—something I find quite appealing.

I learn that he is studying to be a civil engineer at a college in Cusco, but he doesn't think he'll ever have a job as an engineer.

"*Pues, no hay dinero en mi país.* (There is no money in my country.)"
Meanwhile, he has learned English in a course for licensed guides
and works for his father's tour company that will take us on our
horseback trip.

He asks about my family, my husband (he doesn't like Argentine
tourists much), and why he isn't here with me.

I try to explain that he doesn't like camping, but that's not actually true. I can't say it's because he grew up without bathrooms, heat,
running water—because that would make no sense to Raul. I want
to say because he is working—the usual reason why women travel
and husbands stay home—but that would not be accurate either.

The midmorning sun tells us it is time to return to the market.
I follow Raul along an exposed stairway that curves around the
contour of the rock to a terrace below. One more glance back at
the steeply terraced mountainsides leaves me wondering if there is
anywhere in this region that wasn't lived on, cultivated, carved, or
worshipped by the Incas.

As we walk single file along the trail, I wonder if all Peruvians
are proud, like Raul, of their Indian heritage or if their daily struggle is so removed from their history that they can't comprehend or
connect their glorious past with the realities of the present.

Overwhelmed by the industry of the Incas and Peru's past,
I wonder about its future. When George and the millions of
Peruvians like him see the work of their ancestors, are they proud
of their Indian heritage?

How many Latin Americans, I wonder, appreciate—or even
know—what the Aztecs, Mayas, Incas, and pre-Incas accom-
plished? Why do many Latin Americans, including my own
husband, say, "*Que Indio!*" implying something clumsily executed
or dumb? This ideology of superiority seems to be based on the
supposition that the darker your skin, the more likely you are to
be lazy and stupid.

If that were the case, how in the world did the "*Indios*" manage to construct terraces on the steepest mountainsides, dig miles of canals, build aqueducts, and dig tunnels to carry water across ravines and through mountains to neighboring valleys?

In Jose Maria Arguedas's poem, "A Call to Some Doctors," he expresses his frustration with friends and colleagues for their preference for modern solutions to Andean problems.

They say that we don't know anything, that we are backwardness,
that they'll exchange our heads for others, better ones.
They say that some doctors tell this about us; doctors who multiply
in our land, who grow fat here.
What are my brains made of? Of what the flesh of my heart?
The rivers run soaring in their depth. Gold and night, silver and
the fearsome night shape rocks, the walls of the canyons,
the river sounding against them; of that silver and gold night-rock
are my mind, my fingers.
What's there, at river's edge, unknown to you, doctor?
Take out your binoculars, your best lenses. Look, if you can.
Five hundred kinds of flowers of as many kinds of potatoes grow
on the balconies unreached by your eyes; they grow in the earth;
mixed with night and gold, silver and day.
Those five hundred flowers are my brains, my flesh.

Chapter Five

THE PERILOUS PATH
TO PISAC

▼▼▼▼▼▼▼▼▼▼▼▼▼▼

Just after noon, we are back on the bus, descending into the valley for a return trip to Pisac. Raul parks the bus outside of town, and we join throngs of men and women dressed in their traditional Sunday attire. Brad and Patti count six different hat styles, presumably from six different villages. Most of the men wear *chullos* (ear-flap hats), hand knit with many colors of yarn and buttons sewn around the face. Most of the women prefer white straw domes, often decorated with a blue ribbon, the Pisac hat.

"Only pure-blooded Quechua women wear those," Raul says, pointing to a group of women wearing flat, black, felt pancakes with an orange fringe.

We follow him into a large stone enclosure where the only activity seems to be burros munching eucalyptus leaves. *Why are we here?* I wonder, until a man comes out of a deep cavern carrying stacks of pita-like bread.

"Aha, a bakery!

"I buy this for our horse trip in two days," Raul says.

"Won't it be stale by then?" asks Marilyn.

"Pisac bread lasts a week," he replies.

Back on the street, Kate is chatting with two women from New York—the first American tourists we have seen since arriving in Cusco. They compliment Kate on her straw hat, an Orvis catalogue traveler's special.

"Thank you," she replies. "All the ladies in my village wear them."

A maze of stalls filled with pottery, weavings, rugs, sweaters, and jewelry has transformed yesterday's plaza to a handcraft *super-mercado*. Philippe warns us to hang onto cameras and packs.

Kate bargains for a pair of rubber sandals made from tire retreads. For thirty-five cents, she thinks they will make good slippers. Tricia buys a *chicha* jar with two spouts. Raul accompanies us good-naturedly, pointing out necklaces made of tiny shells and beads carved from stones, called *chaquiras,* many of which have been stolen from graves, he tells us.

I am admiring the great carved doors of a church when they fly open, and four men emerge from the dark recesses blowing loud blasts on conch shells, followed by eight men carrying crudely carved wooden staffs with silver inlays that catch the sunlight as they march out into the plaza. They wear black homespun pants, white shirts, and red embroidered vests. Their cone-shaped *chullos* are decorated with buttons, seeds, and shells.

I scurry out of their path, realizing I am in the middle of a ceremony that has changed little since Inca times, when the *varayoqs* (village chieftains) came from neighboring villages to Pisac to discuss crops, wars, ceremonies, and other affairs of the Inca Empire. I wonder what they discuss now.

In the lower part of the market, the produce stalls are closing. Families roll up their belongings in large bundles and tie them on their backs or burros before heading back to their villages. Short, stout women ladle a dirty dishwater-looking liquid from large drums into tin cups and pass it to friends and family, who seem to be quite pleased and a little drunk.

Brad, Patti, Kate, and Tricia watch the process with me.

"What is that stuff?" Kate asks.

"*Chicha*," Brad answers. "Beer made of fermented sweet white corn."

"That's what we drank in Bolivia," Patti adds.

"The women drink as enthusiastically as the men," I observe.

As we leave the marketplace, we find many *chicha*-drinkers lying comatose under the pisonay trees or leaning against the white adobe walls of the *chicherías*.

While waiting for Raul to bring the van closer, I walk a block ahead of our group to a "bus stop" (the "bus" being an open-ended truck where everyone is crammed to the slats with their bulging bundles). Inconspicuous (I hope) between a tree and a broken wall, I observe through my telephoto lens a group of men, all about five feet tall, standing, squatting, or lying in front of a whitewashed wall. Black trousers, rolled to the knees, reveal short, sinewy calves, the result of trudging up and down steep trails with fifty-pound bundles on their backs. Ropes tied in knots hold their worn and broken sandals together. Droopy, sweat-stained felt hats cast a shadow over squinty eyes that stare in an alcoholic stupor. One of the men wears an orange-and-black poncho thrown back off his white shirt. Holding a four-foot-long, carved stanchion shaped much like his own sinewy, bowed legs, he dozes under a felt hat with upturned brim. White tassels hang innocently in front of his closed eyes.

A truck arrives and the men rise, lurch, and stumble, giggling and supporting one another, to the open gate. I move in closer, hoping no one notices which way my camera is aimed. A man on his way to the truck turns from his friends (and me) and pees. A lady comes out from behind a tree and, seeing my camera aimed at the truck, throws a potato at me. I scurry to the safety of the blue van.

With our hats, mantas, rubber shoes, pots, and Pisac bread stored under the seat, Raul drives the bus up a steep hill, leaving the brown adobe walls and faded tile roofs below.

We park on a level lot about halfway up the mountain and set out single file behind Raul, Philippe, and Marilyn on a narrow stone path to the ruins—Brad and Patti chatting merrily ahead of Kate, Tricia, and me. All of us are aware of the deep chasm where the mountain drops off on our left. Abruptly, the trail ends at the head of a flight of stone steps that descend along the edge of the ridge to a terrace below. There's no handrail, just space on either side. I pause and try to look only at my feet, not out at the drop-off to the valley below.

Trail to Pisac Fortress

"Going down is worse than up," Kate reassures us, marching steadfastly down. Tricia stops in front of me, wanting to look back, but afraid to move. "I can't do this," she says.

"Just go slowly. Don't look down," I tell her. I didn't know Tricia had this fear of heights. Perhaps she didn't either. We've skied together with never a glance from a chairlift. "Try one step at a time," I suggest. She stands frozen on the stair. "Tricia, we have to get down this."

"What if I go ahead, and you hang onto my pack."

I know I'll have to pass her on the outside. It's not a maneuver I relish, but I manage to execute it with as much nonchalance as I can muster. Now, her hand on my pack, we proceed downward, slowly, one step at a time.

At the foot of the stairs, the others watch our slow and tentative descent.

"That was awful," Tricia says. "I can't do it again. You don't know what it's like," she says to Kate, who has put her arm around her distressed companion. "Why don't they have handrails?" she asks Raul.

Below and above us, on either side of the mountains, concentric terraces rise from the river a thousand feet below, becoming steeper and narrower and ultimately ending in tiny agricultural balconies. The scattered remains of temples, dwellings, streets, baths, and storage houses cling to the mountainside below us. We continue around the side of the ridge to a section of the trail that crosses a stone buttress protruding from a sheer rock face that drops at least a thousand feet. Ahead is a tunnel. The view out the other side frames cultivated fields in the valley, space, and no path.

Tricia stops, groping for the wall on her right. "Don't make me do this," she pleads. "I know I'm going over the edge. I can feel it." A tear makes its way down taut lips, quickly wiped by a pink tongue.

"You have to," Kate says. "Going back is worse." Holding

Tricia's left hand, Kate leads, and I follow, at a loss for words of encouragement.

Shuffling close to the inside wall, Tricia searches for something hard and permanent with her right hand. When we reach the tunnel, she sighs. "No one ever told me it would be like this," she says, close to tears. I remember that Bill told me some people turn back at this tunnel and never see Pisac. I know Tricia would hate to miss a ruin. Going back would not be easy.

"We're almost there," I encourage her. Inside the tunnel, we stop.

"What if I got down and crawled the rest of the way?" Tricia asks in desperation. Kate looks out of the tunnel at the trail ahead. "It's not that bad," she says. "You can do it. The path turns right, and then we're on a level saddle on the ridge between the terraces below and the ceremonial site just above us. Trust me," Kate says, her clear blue eyes looking deep into Tricia's fear. We round the bend, and Tricia glows with victory.

"That was ghastly," she says. "I could feel myself just falling off into space. I don't know how I did it. I guess my desire to see the ruins—or the absolute horror of turning around and going back—made me go on."

She's laughing now, and I'm relieved, aware that I have brought my friend to this place with no knowledge of the intensity of her fear. Having never experienced acrophobia, I will be more aware of this not uncommon terror throughout our journey in Peru.

Before us, a maze of lichen-covered rectangular stones seems to grow out of the mountainside, suggesting important buildings, private rooms, baths, pathways, and courtyards. A D-shaped wall of splendid Inca masonry curves along the contours of the mountain spur.

"Come here," Raul says, guiding us through a trapezoidal doorway with its overhead lintel firmly in place. We descend a short stairway of perfect dimensions into a courtyard where square blocks seem to grow out of solid stone, so perfectly are they cut and fitted into the natural outcrop.

In the center, a large natural stone with a short granite stump in the middle looks important.

"Ah, the *Inti Huatana* (hitching post of the sun)," Marilyn says. "The only one the Spaniards didn't find is at Machu Picchu." Whether an instrument of solar observation or sun worship, these stone phalluses appear in Inca sites throughout the Andes.

"Those Spaniards," Kate says. "They hacked off the top so the Incas couldn't worship their god, the sun." We turn our attention to the great flights of terraces below us that undulate around the contours of the steep mountainside.

"Look at the stones inserted diagonally like steps up the walls of the terraces," Brad says, pointing. "I always wondered how they got up and down those things."

Raul points to the irrigation channels in the middle of each terrace. "See how the water came down to each level and irrigated the crop before falling to the next?" he says.

We speculate about how many people lived here.

Pisac Terraces

"Hundreds could live here indefinitely," Philippe says. "They grew potatoes, grain, quinoa and maize on the terraces, and there was plenty of water." A spring burbles at my feet and flows into a canal that disappears over the side of the mountain.

"Actually," Raul corrects, "there is no record of many people living here, although this site would be an ideal place to wait out an invasion. The crops grown on the terraces were stored in warehouses for all the empire."

Looking out across the valley, I realize that the Incas could watch the road from Cusco (in case of attack by the Spaniards) as well as the way to the jungle (home of the dreaded Anti tribe). Enemy invasions from either direction (although none occurred here, according to history books) would be seen well in advance.

Kate, looking in the same direction, notices that the Urubamba River meanders in wide sandy swathes across the valley, then runs arrow straight for about three miles near the town of Pisac. "That's strange," she says.

Raul smiles and says, "The Incas did it. They canalized the river so it would not go into their fields. When the river is low, you can see under the water how they built a channel. I have been told it is the largest pre-Columbian canal in the Americas."

All the way back to the hotel and through dinner, we ask, "How many thousands of people cut, carved, and quarried those rocks, then hauled them without horse or cart to the top of the mountain? How did they fit them together? Who was the master architect, the master planner of Pisac? How many thousands built, planted, and cultivated the terraces?"

I look for answers in Peter Frost's handy little orange guidebook, *Exploring Cusco*:

> *"Pisac is the largest fortress-city complex of the Incas, yet early chroniclers mention no word of it. The Spanish knew of it, for*

Urubamba River, straightened by the Incas

certain, as the ruins are visible for miles around. In spite of its awe-inspiring natural defenses, the Incas made no stand here against the Spaniards.

"The City was a classic Inca pucara (citadel), where a large population could endure a siege indefinitely. The entire area was covered with agricultural terraces which served the dual purpose of feeding the city and ringing it with perilous defensive walls. Several springs secured the pucara's water supply."

Frost asks the same question we are all asking, "What was Pisac defending?" And Frost confirms our speculation that the answer lies in the location: "leaving nothing to chance in defending their capital."

On the way to our room, I look across the plaza in front of the hotel at the solid symmetry of an Inca wall, the stones still placed where Manco Inca and his masons put them over five hundred years ago.

Exhausted by the day's assault on all my senses, I throw myself across the bed and succumb to visions of flame-red ponchos spread on the grass in a sunny market, women in round, flat, and domed hats shading their brown faces and broken-toothed smiles—gossiping, bartering, their worn hands weaving ancient patterns into belts and blankets. Throughout the night, I follow a trail of silvery stone walls across fields, over mountains, down paths, and up stairways to palaces, temples, and tombs.

Chapter Six

OLLANTAYTAMBO

▼▼▼▼▼▼▼▼▼▼▼▼▼▼

The following morning, we head down valley to Ollantay-tambo, a village with more ruins. Where the valley narrows between the river on one side and a steep mountainside on the other, I strain to look up at the remains of watchtowers, their remaining stones blending with the tawny cliffs three thousand feet above the road. Abandoned dwellings lie open to the elements, revealing the complexity of their structure but none of their secrets. I wish we were in a convertible so I could look up.

The paved road becomes an Inca road of inlaid stones that leads to a plaza where we park under a Coca-Cola sign. Two men in red-patterned ponchos chat on a stone bench, watching us through the bobbing black tassels of their round red hats. Raul greets them in Quechua, buys them each a beer, and joins them on the bench.

Marilyn has informed us that Ollanta (as she calls it) is the only village in Peru that exists much as the Incas laid it out hundreds of years ago. Each *cancha* (block) houses three or four families and their livestock. They share a yard and have a common entrance through the high walls that protect them on all four sides. These walls support the structures of clay and thatch (and sometimes tin) that house the present-day inhabitants.

Eager to inspect Inca urban planning, Kate, Tricia, and I enter a street of inlaid stones between two ten-foot-high walls—just wide enough for three people to walk abreast. Down the center of the street, we note the gutter that once carried water from the dwellings to a larger canal that ran beneath the plaza to the river. We hope this form of waste removal has been improved upon since Inca times.

Street of stone and running water

Through an open entry to one of the *canchas,* I see children playing, laundry drying on warm rocks, women weaving on backstrap
looms in the shade of a tree, and free-range chickens, goats, and burros
roaming about the piles of corn in search of leaves to eat. From another
open entrance, a donkey steps daintily into the street, and a fat pig
waddles around the corner and enters the doorway of a neighboring
cancha, like a neighbor dropping in for a visit or to borrow some sugar.

We have been walking for fifteen minutes without saying a
word, engrossed in our shared and separate discoveries. Patti and
Brad stand in a trapezoidal doorway under a wrought-iron sign
that says, "*Ataúds, todo tamaños buena calidad.* (Caskets, all sizes
and fine quality.)"

Together, we start down a long, straight, narrow street toward
the square. A small herd of black cattle come *clip-clopping* out of a
side street behind us. As they approach with increasing speed, Kate
and I step back into an empty niche.

"Yikes, we'll be trampled!" Patti shouts as Brad pulls her into
a doorway. Tricia, sauntering on ahead, stops to take a picture with
her back turned. We yell at her, but she doesn't hear us. When she
finally turns around and sees the herd bearing down on her, she has
no choice but to outrun the trotting herd into the square.

The men in the red ponchos giggle behind their tassels, and
Raul stands to watch Tricia's escape, not sure if he should join in
the laughter or rescue the fleeing Tricia. Breathless, she steps aside
and watches the cows saunter over to a patch of grass at the edge
of the square.

"Were you scared?" Patti asks Tricia when we join her.

"I didn't have time to be scared, just wanted to get the hell out
of there," she says, laughing. Marilyn and Philippe motion for us
to follow them to the ruins, and Raul joins us.

"Who are your friends?" I ask, as we follow an Inca canal on
a path from the town to the base of the ruins.

"We call them *huayruros*," he replies. "It is a Quechua word for a red berry that grows along the Inca Trail. The men from this town work as porters on the Inca trail, and when they walk in the mountains, they look like berries under their red capes."

He smiles in their direction, and as we follow Kate and Tricia across the square, he says, "*Tu eres una mujer para hacer el Camino Inca conmigo.* (You are a woman to walk the Inca Trail with me.)"

Glowing with newfound confidence in my athletic ability, I wonder if I could really do that—four days walking, straight up for two of them, to sixteen thousand feet, then on through the Sun Gate and down to Machu Picchu. I envision Raul leading the way up the Inca Trail with ten *huayruros* as my personal support team.

We cross the Patacancha River and stop under a granite lintel that spans the ten-foot-high entrance to the ruins—a fitting overture to the two hundred steps we must climb to reach the heart of yet another great Inca fortress.

Marilyn and Philippe lead the way up through a vertical community of apartments, elaborate baths, gardens, temples, storage areas, small plots for grazing animals, soldiers' barracks, and a jail—all interconnected by level paths, canals, corridors, and scary overlooks.

Philippe shows us a carved niche on a promontory two thousand feet above the river, and tells us that a condemned person stood there with his hands tied to knobs at shoulder length. "He would eventually die of exposure or starvation," Philippe says, gazing morosely over the edge.

Kate pulls her dark glasses down on her nose and rolls her eyes.

Across the valley and above the town on an inaccessible mountainside (there are no stairs that I can see), a long stone building appears to be empty but still intact. Marilyn thinks it was a place for the sacred women. Raul disputes this theory.

"The Incas liked their women. They would never put them so far from their palace. More likely it was a warehouse where no one could get to it," he says with some logic.

One of the nice things about pre-conquest Inca history is that nothing was written, so you can more or less make up your own version. If Raul were an Inca, he wouldn't put his women over there.

We climb higher, skirting the ruins to the side of the mountain that looks down on the Urubamba River and across to the quarry that was allegedly the source of all the granite that lies above and below us. Again, we ask: How did mere mortals transport these three-hundred-ton blocks from a quarry twenty miles away? We know they had to cross a hanging vine bridge over a wild and dangerous river, climb the steep trail to the quarry, fetch the giant boulders, and return up an even steeper slope to where we stand now. Huge cut boulders lie strewn about in a corn field below—eternal evidence that some great stones and great men, on their way from the quarry, rolled down the mountainside and into the river.

I RETURN TO THE FRONT OF THE RUIN that looks out over the car park, the ancient town of Ollantaytambo and across a large flat plain where a famous battle was fought between the Spaniards and the Incas.

After the Spaniards arrived in Cusco in 1533, Hernando Pizarro and his men lived relatively peacefully while Manco Inca acted as their puppet, but in 1536 Manco decided to rebel. Thousands of Indians were killed when he lost a long and bloody battle at the fort of Sacsayhuaman, outside of Cusco. Manco retreated to his palace in Yucay in the Urubamba Valley. Since Yucay was not well fortified, he moved to Ollantaytambo, where he continued his rebellious raids on the Spaniards. Pizarro, annoyed by this pesky guerilla, decided to get rid of Manco and his loyal followers and put an end to the raids.

In *The Conquest of the Incas*, John Hemming wrote:

> *"With seventy horse and thirty foot and a large contingent of native auxiliaries, the Spaniards fought their way upriver from Cusco to Ollantaytambo."*

They had to cross the river five or six times, fending off Indian attackers at each ford. At last they arrived at Ollantaytambo, only to find an unheard-of fortress looming above them. One of the soldiers quoted by Hemming says, *When we reached tambo, we found it so well fortified that it was a horrifying sight.* Archers from the nearby jungle had been recruited to rain down arrows from every direction on men and horses as they stood on the plain below (now a parking lot).

According to one of Pizarro's men:

> *They do not know what is meant by flight, for they continue to fight with arrows even when dying.*

Using accounts from Spanish soldiers, and sometimes quoting them directly, Hemming wrote:

> *"The town was full of these archers, firing from every terrace. Across the stream were Inca slingers. The Indians were thus fighting from three sides: some from the hillside, others from the far bank of the river, and the rest from the town. . . . The Inca was in the fortress itself with many well-armed warriors. A single flight of steps led up to the citadel. The gate at its foot had been sealed with a fieldstone wall through which an Indian could pass only on all fours. Two of the*

older conquistadores bravely rode their horses up against the walls of the town, but, 'it was amazing to see the arrows that rained down on them as they returned, and to hear the shouting.' Another group of horsemen tried to attack the terraces below the citadel. But the defendants 'hurled down so many boulders and fired so many slingshots that, even had we been many more Spaniards than we were, we would all have been killed.'"

Pizarro's men were forced to retreat and regroup in the flat plain beyond the fortress. However, the Incas then used water as a weapon. Through a previously devised system of channels and ditches, the Indians had diverted the Patacancha River. They had only to pull a few dikes to flood the plains and mire the horsemen in a muddy bog with water rising rapidly to their girths.

Hemming wrote:

"Night fell, and the Spaniards tried to slide away under cover of darkness, leaving their tents pitched beneath Ollantaytambo. But the column of defeated horsemen was observed 'and the Indians came down upon them with a great cry . . . grabbing the horses' tails.' They attacked us with great fury at a river crossing, carrying burning torches . . . There is one thing about these Indians: when they are victorious they are demons in pressing it home, but when they are fleeing they are like wet hens. Since they were now following up a victory, seeing us return, they pursued with great spirit. They littered the road back with thorny agave spines which crippled the horses."

Ollantaytambo was left in peace until a year later when Pizarro returned with greater numbers, forcing Manco to retreat farther into the jungle to Vilcabamba, where he eventually fought his last battle.

Now, on the plain below us, an invasion of a different sort is taking place. Vans and buses, parked in neat rows, bring tourists to stare in awe at the fortress rising above them, and descendants of the Incas attack with rugs and weavings, T-shirts and pottery.

The more I see and learn of this country—its ruins, its civilizations, its people—the more I want to know. Most ancient civilizations have been chronicled, studied, and explained to the point where all one can do is read and learn what others have discovered. I know that Peru will always be studied and analyzed, but will it ever be completely explained or totally discovered? I hope not, for the challenge of unsolved mysteries offers the opportunity to make one's own discoveries.

Halfway down the knee-cracking stairs, Raul invites me to the edge of a nearby cliff overlooking the train tracks where they disappear, along with the Urubamba River into the jungle.

"Cuando estoy aqui en Ollanta, siento mi vida pasada. Siento que soy Inca. (When I am here in Ollanta, I feel my past life. I feel that I am Inca)," he confides.

I, too, feel some inexplicable connection to this place, and at the same time, a connection with Raul. We watch a train pass on its way to Machu Picchu. In a week we will be there.

Chapter Seven

RETURN TO CUSCO AND TO THE WOMEN ON THE CALLE DEL SOL

▼▼▼▼▼▼▼▼▼▼▼▼▼▼▼▼▼

O n the way back to Cusco, we stop for lunch at a hillside restaurant with a fine view and frightening food. A chunk of greasy
pigskin, its black hairs still attached, floats on the surface of an
oily soup.

Marilyn insists we order *cui* (guinea pig). It looks like a dead
rat splayed flat on a bed of rice and potatoes.

"It will take lots of beer to get that down," Brad remarks.

I eat just enough not to insult the proprietor.

"*No comes mas?*" Raul asks. "*No comes la cabecita?* (No more?
Aren't you going to eat the little head?)"

I pass the carcass to him. He bites off an ear with his gleaming
white teeth and nibbles contentedly until all that is left are two tiny
teeth and a forehead.

BY MIDAFTERNOON WE ARE BACK at the hotel, the spoils of the Andean markets displayed on the white llama fur bedspread—red ponchos, multicolored belts and blankets, faded vests, coca bags, earflap hats, pre-Columbian (we hope) pots, and a variety of silver adornments. All these treasures plus our civilian clothes will be stored in the hotel for a week while we travel by horseback along the Royal Road of the Inca over the Andes to Machu Picchu.

Kate eyes the orange canvas saddlebag at the foot of her bed. "This goes on the horse?" She looks at me over her glasses balanced on the tip of her nose.

"Yes. Bill says to put everything you might want during the ride in the saddle bags. Our sleeping bags, ground cloths, Ensolite pads, and whatever we can roll in there, like long underwear and extra clothes, go in separate duffels with the pack animals."

"That means I need to pack my down parka, rainwear, camera stuff," Tricia says, making a mental list, as she piles these items at one end of the bed.

"I'm taking first-aid supplies, mosquito lotion, toilet paper, sunglasses, flashlight . . . what else?" Kate thinks aloud.

"My new hat," I announce, pulling out a floppy felt hat that I bought in a shop around the corner the first day in Cusco. "It's reversible, re-shapeable, foldable, and waterproof."

"We should all get them," Tricia says. "It will be our tribal hat. Where did you buy it?"

"I'll show you," I say, and we grab our packs and head for the door.

"How much?" Kate asks.

"About three dollars."

We meet Brad and Patti on the stairs, and they join us on the tribal hat quest.

I lead them to the shop and show them the pile of rather misshapen, whitish, cone-like felt hats. Tricia picks one out, bends and turns up the brim, adds a colorful band, and pulls it down to her ears. Approved by shoppers, shopkeepers, and the tribe, she pays and makes her way through the piles of ponchos, rugs, and alpaca sweaters to see what Kate has selected. Patti and Kate are pleading and wheedling for a quantity discount.

"We buy three . . . *tres? Por favor?*"

The shopkeeper stands firm. Patti and Brad pay the equivalent of three dollars.

Kate declines—too expensive.

During the heat of the bargaining, I bid my friends *adiós* and leave the shop to walk to the Plaza de Armas. The late afternoon sun casts a golden glow on the cathedral, Inca walls, Spanish churches, shops, arcades, and palaces and intensifies the brilliant yellow blossoms of huge *retama* (Scotch broom) bushes in the center of the square, where I walk toward the imposing cathedral.

One of the finest cathedrals in all South America, it was built on the site of an Inca palace. The Incas laid the foundations in 1550, but during its hundred years of construction, architectural stages, and artistic embellishments, it passed from Spanish colonial to baroque to renaissance.

I enter the church through a side door and stand in awe of the massive solid silver altar. Behind it, I find the original hand-carved wooden altar, one of many masterpieces of Andean wood carving.

The Incas, commissioned by the Spaniards to paint religious scenes for the church, added their own interpretations of a religion they must have found puzzling. In a painting of the Last Supper, Christ and the apostles are about to dine on *cui*—just like we had for lunch. In another, the artists, who doubted babies could fly, painted the winged cherubs clinging to a curtain surrounding a very pregnant Virgin Mary.

As I leave the cathedral, a thunderous *clang* sounds from a tower above me, its tone reverberating across the square, the city, and perhaps the entire Inca Empire. It is the Maria Angola, the largest bell in South America.

When Jose Maria Arquedas visited Cusco with his father and heard the Maria Angola for the first time, he described his wonder and emotion in *Rios Profundos* (*Deep Rivers*):

> "'The Maria Angola,' I cried.
>
> "The world must have been changed into gold at that moment—I, too, as well as the walls and the city, the towers, and the facades I had seen.
>
> "I knew the voice of the bell carried a distance of five leagues. I thought the plaza would explode with sound. But the vibrations expanded slowly, at spaced intervals—growing stronger, piercing the elements, transmuting everything into that Cusco music that opened the doors of memory."

With five more chimes resonating off the stones of Inca palaces and down the shadowy streets of Cusco, I cross the square in the fading light of evening. Cusco feels good to me as I walk down the Calle del Sol to the hotel. Indian women sit cross-legged in their nests of sweaters, rugs, belts, and ponchos. They nod as I pass, speaking shyly, *"Buenas noches, señora."*

Some of them are eating supper—rice and soup in a tin cup. Others nurse babies and gossip with their neighbors.

On our many excursions up and down this street, Kate, Tricia, and I have stopped to admire their wares and debate over a sweater or a rug. Gentle and direct, they laugh at Kate's attempts to drive their prices down. They warn us to be careful of pickpockets, to put our money away.

When we returned earlier today from the Urubamba Valley, they seemed happy to see us, asked us what we bought and how much we paid, and commented on whether it was a bargain or not (usually not).

The women on the Calle del Sol arrive early every afternoon, spread their wares around them, and stay until the last tourists have retreated to their hotels for the night. On Sundays, they travel by local bus to the markets at Pisac and Chinchero in the Urubamba Valley, where they barter for new goods, trade, and sell to tourists. They are hard-working, savvy business women, experts in purchasing, marketing, and sales.

Kate and Tricia remind me that they are poor, that their babies suffer from respiratory diseases and malnutrition, that they lack heat and sanitation in their houses, and that they are often hungry and cold. We know their husbands get drunk and beat them. They have every reason to be miserable, resentful, and filled with despair. They don't seem that way to me. The women, especially my friends on the Calle del Sol, seem to possess some nobility of spirit that transcends their poverty.

AT DINNER IN OUR HOTEL, BILL introduces us to three new members of our group who arrived today from Lima. Judy, a tall, slender, twenty-eight-year-old nurse from Santa Fe, New Mexico, speaks Spanish and likes horses. She is warm, enthusiastic, and curious about all that we have seen and done. I know immediately I will like her.

Lauren, Judy's younger cousin from the Midwest, has accentuated her dark brown eyes with the careful application of mascara, and her deep red lips leave a perfect imprint on her napkin, as she places it in her lap and tells us about hiking in Switzerland last year, where Judy decided that Peru would be their next destination.

Don, also in his twenties, lives in San Francisco. He appears frail, compared to the rest of us, and I wonder how he will fare on this trip. Nevertheless, he has no trepidations about horses or what lies ahead.

Kate encourages them to go buy our tribal hat, and tells them where she bought hers for a dollar less than what we paid.

Later, I lie in bed with the light still on, my senses filled with Peru—its Inca past, its puzzling present, and all the sights, sounds, smells that were so foreign a week ago and now seem familiar, part of who I am. For the first time in days, I think about my family and my children—would they love this adventure? Would my husband?

Kate, staring at the ceiling that she's already warned us might cave in on us at any moment, says, "You know I don't like horses, and they don't like me."

"Bill says these horses are pretty tame, more like a conveyance," I try to reassure her.

"I sure hope so, because I've never had a good experience on a horse," she says. "Do you remember the horse show in Squaw Valley when one broke loose, ran out the gate, and ran over me?"

"Of course, I'll never forget it," I say, as the memory of that terrible freak accident comes vividly back. Kate had crossed the paddock to climb a fence when a frightened, riderless animal galloped out of the ring, knocked her over, and must have kicked her head. Normally, horses don't like anything, least of all humans, under their feet, and they will do anything to avoid that. Kate was unconscious for a few hours and still remembers very little about her husband arriving on the scene or the ambulance ride to the hospital.

"That was so bad," I say, sitting up and looking at Kate. "A freak accident like that can influence you for a lifetime. I've never had anything but good relationships with horses."

Tricia, who has been listening to our conversation, says, "That's because you lived on a ranch, and you probably had well-trained horses."

"Not necessarily," I say, remembering some scary runaways. "But I did have a childhood of good experiences in all kinds of situations on many different horses."

"I'll survive," Kate says. "It will all be worth it when we get off the horses and arrive at Machu Picchu."

"I haven't ridden a horse for years," Tricia says. "I'm much more afraid of heights than horses."

"Bill told me the horses are sure-footed and have been over this trail many times," I say, hoping he is right.

I know my two friends are strong, independent, and fearless in their own environment, but I feel a twinge of responsibility mixed with keen anticipation for tomorrow's adventure.

Chapter Eight

TRUCK TO TRAILHEAD

▼▼▼▼▼▼▼▼▼▼▼▼▼▼▼

Stars fade in a pale sky, as the morning sun spreads its warm cloak across the highest Andean peaks above Cusco. On the street outside our hotel, crowded by day with vendors from surrounding villages, a young boy stands alone, holding an armload of woven belts. I climb into the back of the truck, crawl up and over saddle bags, crates of cooking gear, boxes of food, tents, saddles, and blankets to a perch in the corner, and nestle into my down parka. Kate and Tricia choose the opposite corner, eyeing with suspicion a collapsible dining table tied to the side.

Bill climbs past us to a seat on a board mounted atop the cabin. Marilyn and Philippe join him. Judy and Lauren claim their spots between us. Brad and Patti climb a stack of orange canvas crates on the right side and settle on a lumpy duffel bag, where they'll have a view and can hang on to the top slats of the truck. Don chooses to stand on the floor in the back of the truck, hanging on to a rod that extends from the top of the cab to the rear of the truck bed. He abandons this immediately when the truck starts off up a steep, bumpy street and heads out of Cusco—gears grinding down at each hairpin turn. Raul and his uncle Jaime, our cook, shift boxes and two guitars around to make a seat for Don.

An exhilarating breeze carries the sharp odors of scotch broom, burning cedar, and kerosene as we speed across the Limatambo Valley. In roadside farmyards, men, women and children wrapped in scruffy alpaca sweaters feed their pigs, chase straying chickens, and bring the cows in to milk. *Campesinos* leading their burros, loaded with produce, make their daily journey along the road to the market town of Izcuchaca.

We stop there to buy bananas, rum, and pisco. Stout ladies in blue dresses with stiff white top hats watch us from the side of the road. Their children climb the sides of the truck to sell us boiled eggs and potatoes. Philippe, imposing and arrogant on top of the truck, shoos them away with a disdainful, "*Vayanse! Abajo!*"

We climb down the ladder to the street, dispersing into small shops and along the main thoroughfare, while Philippe remains on guard. Kate disappears into a low stone building with a tin roof, hoping to find yet another market filled with ponchos, a *cinta* to wrap around her waist, another alpaca sweater—even cheaper than the four she left behind in Cusco. Tricia and I prepare to greet her and examine her latest purchase, but she's walking toward us empty-handed, lips pursed as if she just ate a sour plum.

"It was not the kind of market I thought," she says. "All dead, bloody animals—even dogs, I think. The stench was unbelievable! I took a picture of a dead cow lying on a table. Her big brown eyes were staring at me."

"Are you sure she was dead?"

"Her head had no skin."

We are interrupted by Bill, who has just heard on a radio that a bomb in the tourist train from Machu Picchu exploded in the Cusco station last night.

"Was it the Shining Path?" Kate asks. "Was anyone hurt or killed?"

"They don't know," Bill replies. "I don't know who else it would be."

"I thought Senderos didn't attack tourists," Tricia half questions.

"Normally they don't. I guess no one knows what they'll do."

Raul joins us. "*Murieron cuatro turistas Alemanes.* (Four German tourists were killed)," he announces.

"Oh, my God," Tricia exclaims and translates for Kate. "Surely this will make the foreign newspapers."

I look at Bill for guidance. "What will our families think? They know we were in Cusco. They might think we were on the train."

"And they know we are going to Machu Picchu on the train . . . maybe we should call them and let them know we're okay," Kate suggests.

"We can't," Bill responds, thrusting his hands into the waist of tight faded jeans. "There isn't a phone anywhere until we get back to Cusco next week."

Raul suggests we send a message with a phone number for his father to call in the US. The truck driver can take it back to Cusco tonight after he lets us off at the trailhead.

This seems a satisfactory solution, and we climb into the truck to tell the rest of the group. Pat writes down names and numbers of our families and her daughter's number to call in Los Angeles.

All cares are soon forgotten, as once more we speed along the open road. Mud farm houses surrounded by dogs, children, and heaps of well-used farm tools line the road. Most of the roofs are thatch, but the more affluent farmers have tile roofs, and they bless this achievement by placing a broken *chicha* pot, a ceramic bull, or a shiny weather vane on top. All these adornments bring good luck to the owners and make festive silhouettes in the morning sky.

It's planting time in this high mountain valley, and just as in Inca times, the men are plowing a single row with a foot plow. Women and children follow behind, breaking up the earth with hope and a hoe.

Brown, yellow, ochre, sienna—tones of earth and grain—cover the undulating terrain in every direction. On the horizon, sunbeams search through windswept clouds, suddenly spotlighting a white mountain that seems to float, disconnected, above the horizon.

"That's Soray," Bill tells us. "It's only nineteen thousand feet."

Impatient clouds erase it from the sky.

I know Salcantay is there somewhere. The clouds part again, framing a more distant, much grander white peak.

"That's it," Bill says, pointing. "Salcantay, the second highest peak in Peru—'the wild one' in Quechua."

The mountain I first saw in a slide show in my living room in California, then again from the plane as we landed in Cusco, is finally within reach. From now on, it will play hide-and-seek, looming and vanishing behind peaks and clouds until the day we ride to its base.

On top of the truck, I have a 360-degree view of Peru. I feel good about this trip. It is a tour, but not an *organized* tour. In fact, all attempts to be organized have been foiled by late starts, unexpected circumstances, and personal inclinations.

Although we left home with a printed itinerary of daily excursions—to the Urubamba Valley, Chinchero and Pisac markets, Ollantaytambo, and "free afternoons for shopping in Cusco"—Bill has frequently asked us what we would like to see or do next, and we have found ourselves inventing a new itinerary based on personal whims and wishes. With limited knowledge of our options and no idea how to execute them, we haven't been able to respond with any viable alternatives. Kate has observed that at times, Bill seems to follow as much as to lead. We don't know if this is due to circumstances out of his control, an effort to please all of us, or just ineptitude. Kate suspects the latter.

For example, when Bill asked, "Do you want to go to the market or the ruins?" Tricia preferred the ruins, Kate the market, and I was content with either, hoping to go to both.

When he asked our opinion on eating in a cheap local place with questionable food or a clean place with predictable food and a bathroom, Kate would most likely choose the cheap place. Tricia and I would be fine with either, and Kate would accuse me of always preferring the more luxurious, assuming my suburban upbringing had not prepared me for the questionable hygiene and uncertainty of the Third World. I would defend myself by describing my "honeymoon" living with my in-laws in Patagonia in winter and traveling over miles of dirt roads without a town or a soul in sight.

If Bill asked us which market, ruin, street, or road to take, we asked Marilyn—after all, she "*did* the Inca Trail." Others in the group added their opinions to Marilyn's and Bill's, and eventually we agreed on a plan. Often that plan was adjusted or abandoned. This modus operandi had Kate exasperated, Tricia annoyed, and the rest of us tired and confused.

After a week of traveling with my two friends, I have learned that Kate dislikes the insecurity of not being properly prepared— not knowing how much film, toilet paper, money, sunscreen, Pepto-Bismol, and layers of clothing she'll need. Tricia tells us both to "go with the flow." Oddly, I find myself perversely disappointed when we actually do what we started out to do.

The truck bounces along a dirt road, creating a cloud of dust that obliterates the world and all itineraries left behind. The open country ahead offers new freedom, not just to "go with the flow," but to accept the challenge of change and the opportunity to pursue it without fear of the consequences.

Winding slowly now through hilly country, we descend into a deep valley. Terraced fields, rich with citrus, avocados, walnut trees, and vegetables, bask in the sun behind wooden corrals, barns, and houses.

We stop for lunch at Tarahuasi (old house), a lonely ruin set in a narrow crease of the green mountainside. An Inca wall stretches across a field for three hundred feet. Copper-colored lichens on stones the size of watermelons shimmer in the sun. Although haphazard in pattern, the octagonal stones fit like a jigsaw puzzle. The top of the wall is perfectly level. A smaller wall with man-size niches stretches across the back field.

We open our picnic crate and stretch out on the grass in the shade of the wall. Suddenly, a local farmer and self-proclaimed curator comes out of the ruin and stands like a priest on a rock. He recites in Quechua the tale of Pachacutec, ninth Inca and great builder of walls and palaces. Jaime and Raul translate into English.

His booming voice tells us that Pachacutec (1438–1471/2) lived here and guarded this valley and its route to Cusco, that

Lichen-covered Inca Wall, Tarahuasi

Pachacutec was a brave and intelligent king. He conquered tribes in all directions, enlarging the empire more than any other Inca. When he saw the great buildings of Tiahuanaco on the southern shore of Lake Titicaca, he was so impressed by the quality of the stonework that he ordered his men to use this construction method in Cusco and throughout the empire. Much of what still stands today in Cusco, the Urubamba valley, and outlying villages was built during Pachacutec's reign.

The orator on the rock finishes his lecture, informing us that Tarahuasi is considered one of the four corners of *Tawantinsuyu* (the Inca Empire), and that *Pachakutiq* in Quechua means "he who remakes the world."

On the way back to the truck, Jaime tells me that the hills around us once produced a tomato crop that supplied all of Peru and were exported to other Andean countries. "Now they produce barely enough for local consumption," he says.

I ask about a large house in good repair, standing at the entrance to the ruins.

"The owner lives in Lima," Jaime says. "The local *campesinos* plant and harvest their crops and live on what they grow or trade locally. It's too far for them to travel to the market in Izcuchaca or Cusco." We pause by the truck to admire the seldom-visited estate of "someone who lives in Lima."

Raul says it was once the home of the majordomo who owned all the land in this valley.

I ask what happened to him and if things are better now.

"*No, pués,*" Jaime replies, and explains that in the 1960s, under the land reform laws implemented by General Velasco, much of the agricultural land was taken from the old landholders and given to the *campesinos*. The result was a tremendous loss in Peru's agricultural output, as most of the Indian population has let the land deteriorate until it produces only what the family needs to survive.

Jaime and Raul, like most Peruvians, feel that the Indians are lazy and content with subsistence farming. Raul says they have no money to buy seeds, tools, and fertilizer. They have no way to transport their goods to markets. "The government should help them," he says.

I wonder if their predicament is influenced by something historically more complex than laziness. Subsistence under the care of an overlord has been a way of life to these people for centuries. Under Inca rule, the Indians possessed only what the state allowed. They were given land and livestock, and their allotment of cloth, food, and tools was stored in warehouses to be given out freely whenever droughts, floods, or prolonged wars made it necessary. The workers kept only what they needed, similar to the way they live today.

In Inca times, families were born to a trade and remained in it for generations. Everyone worked: blind people, cripples, children, and old people. *Mita*, a form of social security, was paid in services such as preparing for wars, acting as soldiers, building and caring for temples, or working in one's community. There was no "early retirement," no shirking, no disobedience.

Since there was no money, no poverty, and no need to steal, there was very little crime. However, transgressions such as murder, theft, adultery, drunkenness, and laziness were considered actions against the Inca and his deities and were punishable by anything from public reprimand to mutilation to death by stoning or pushing a person off a cliff. There were no prisons, so punishment was swift and usually public, as the purpose was to teach a lesson to both culprit and society.

As I climb into the truck, I wonder how many years it takes to unlearn what your ancestors did for centuries and become a capitalist.

The truck lurches and sways downhill, creating a cloud of dust all around us—in our eyes, in our shirts. Those who have bandanas tie them over their mouths. Ruts left from the muddy season bounce us from hole to hole, while the grinding of downshifting gears and rattle of loosened crates announce our progress through a landscape devoid of plants, animals, or humans. Sun-scorched red clay mountains form a barrier between us and the green rolling hills that descend to the Pacific coast. Somewhere in a deep gorge below flows the mighty Apurímac River ("The Great Speaker" in Quechua).

If it could speak now, it would tell of the victorious return to Cusco by Inca warriors who crossed high above its deathly roar on a fifteen-thousand-foot suspension bridge of woven vines, carrying their emperor, Pachacutec, on a litter and followed by supply trains of llamas, conquered *Chanca* prisoners and treasures for the Inca. It would tell you how the *chaca camuyoc* (keeper of bridges) warned the Incas of the approach of the Spaniards, and how they burned the bridge, and how the Spaniards remarkably forded the river and continued to pursue them across the plains to Cusco.

A new bridge was constructed and made famous by Thornton Wilder in *The Bridge of San Luis Rey*. After linking the Inca Trail from Cusco to the north for five centuries, the bridge collapsed in 1890.

An abrupt right-hand turn takes us up a road shaded by thorny trees, whose low branches send us diving and ducking into a bed of boxes, packs, and crates. We pass grassy green fields surrounded by remnants of stone walls, slowing down as a school and a church come into view. Crowds of children greet us, their little hands reaching up to us, as they plead for "*misqui, misqui, dulces, caramelos* (candy)."

This is Mollepata—the last outpost of civilization until we reach Santa Teresa in six days on the other side of the Andes. Bill inquires where he can buy firewood and sets off to find it.

Philippe, ever vigilant, tells the children to stay away from the truck. Brown eyes stare openly at us from a discreet distance while we climb over the sides and congregate at the intersection of the only two roads in town.

Truck stop Mollepata

Bill returns with a thin man in a sweat-stained gray flannel shirt and jeans, one cheek bulging with coca leaves. Jaime and Raul shake his hand respectfully and introduce us to Cerilio. Together they supervise the loading of the firewood, which has been delivered by two burros with their twelve-year-old master.

"How long will we be here?" Pat asks no one in particular.

"I don't know," Brad answers, "but we'd better not stray far from the truck. I'd hate to be left in this godforsaken place."

"Now what happens?" Kate asks.

"*Los arrieros viven aqui. Tienen caballos.*" Jaime answers. (The wranglers live here. They have horses.) Bill is negotiating through Cerilio how many horses, pack animals, and *arrieros* we need, and Jaime and Raul have gone to find Antonín, the head *arriero*.

Pat and Brad stand by, hands in pockets, trying to assess the situation. Kate wonders aloud if this couldn't have been all arranged previously. Tricia laughs, consoling Kate with the fact that there are no phones here, and these *arriero* guys probably don't live in town.

Sitting on a pile of rocks by the roadside, I watch the scene, wondering what Osvaldo would think of this. *Arrieros*, much like gauchos in his country or cowboys in mine, are tough, taciturn, independent, and fiercely protective of their livestock. I recall the words of an Argentine folk song Osvaldo sings, accompanied by his guitar:

Por los arenas bailan los remolinos
El sol jeuga en la cuna del pedregal
Perdido en la magia de los caminos
El arriero va
El arriero va

Las penas y las vaquitas
Se van por la misma senda
Las penas son de nosotros
Las vaquitas son ajenas

....

Over the sands dance the tumbleweeds.
The sun plays in a bed of rocks
And lost in the magic of the trails
The arriero goes.
The arriero goes.

The sorrows and the cows
Follow the same path.
The sorrows are ours.
The cows are someone else's.

"Let's see where that road goes," Judy suggests. "It'll just take a few minutes to climb to the top." I follow Judy and Lauren up the hill, avoiding the stream that runs down the middle and the yapping dogs that leap from behind fences fortified by broken coke bottles. Dwellings constructed with scraps of wood and metal line the road, and I feel the eyes of mute observers watching us from their doorways. No one greets us.

At the top of the hill, an empty plaza in front of a church awaits the next market or fiesta day. Low ramshackle buildings, most of them shops or bars, face the plaza. Salcantay, pure and white, appears on the wrong horizon.

"Hey, isn't that mountain supposed to be over there?" Lauren asks, pointing in the opposite direction. My instinctual compass is always out of order in the Southern Hemisphere. North "feels" south to me.

"I guess not," Judy replies. "'Cause that's the desert and the ocean over that way, and the mountains are over there."

"Look, Jaime and Raul went in that restaurant over there," Judy says, and we cross the road, hesitating at the door. When our eyes adjust to the dark interior, we see the bar is full of men.

"Come on," Judy urges, "let's have a beer."

We enter, and all conversation stops. Dark eyes with dilated pupils stare at us from dark-skinned faces that reveal no emotion. Not sure whether to retreat or hold my ground, I look to Judy and her friends for a sign. They have no retreat in mind and walk confidently to the bar, all eyes following them.

Since I am about twice their age, I feel conspicuous but, thankfully, less desirable. Two men near the door are talking in Quechua, and I recognize the word "*gringas*."

There's something about their demeanor that makes me uncertain whether we are in danger or just intruding in their private world. Raul emerges from a stinking bathroom with no door.

"*Chicas*, what are you doing here?" he asks. He pays for his beer and ushers us out the door. "There was a bad fight in there last night. Somebody was killed."

"Killed? My God," Lauren says, hurrying down the path behind Raul.

"*Que mujeres bolludas,*" he mutters to himself.

That's exactly what Osvaldo would have said, I think.

"Women don't go in bars," he informs us, "unless they are looking for trouble." The three younger women are surprised at this old-fashioned attitude. I am not.

Back at the truck we meet the chief *arriero*, Antonín, whose head is wrapped in a dirty bandage. Last night his father-in-law hit him with a shovel in the bar we just visited—evidently the result of drunken accusations of infidelity.

The truck, now loaded with firewood and two new passengers, stops to pick up an extra driver who will pilot us through the maze of roads, streams, and rock walls that mark the boundaries of fields and farmlands. Ducking low branches and gripping the center pole, we lurch up a dirt road, ford streams, get stuck, get out and walk, and get stuck again. The road becomes a cow path and eventually disappears, but the driver seems to know the way to our destination at the edge of a deep canyon, where he turns around and leaves us.

From this point on, we will have no contact with civilization until we reach the village of Santa Teresa on the Urubamba River on the other side of the mountains. There we will board the train that follows the river to Machu Picchu, where we have reservations in the hotel at the ruins—a destination that seems like the other side of the world right now.

Raul and Jaime set to work erecting the crew tent, while the rest of us rummage through piles of gear to identify packs and sleeping bags.

Bill gathers us for a clinic on tent assembly, bathroom etiquette (a hole will be dug in an appropriate place for a toilet; a roll of toilet paper hanging on a branch signifies that the toilet is unoccupied), and general hygiene: "Wash your hands in chlorine and water after going to the bathroom and before handling food. Drinking water will be either boiled or purified with iodine."

Soon our small green tents line the sides of the road, facing west toward the setting sun. The deep valley drops into dusky shadows below, and I can see a father and his son bringing two cows home from a field across the way.

I sit alone on my sleeping bag, absorbed in the stillness of the moment, trying to describe it in my diary. Suddenly, Cerilio steps out of the bushes three feet away. His buckshot black eyes stare from behind an armload of firewood.

"*Gringa!*" he declares. I wonder if this is an accusation. Perhaps he doesn't like me—or perhaps it is merely a salutation. He shuffles off to the fire.

After a dinner of charcoal-burned steak and squashed apple pie, we huddle close to a small fire. Philippe, sitting on a portable toilet seat, strums a guitar and sings sad Ecuadorian love songs. He has a lovely voice, and his Spanish is flawless. I wonder how someone so romantic and so familiar with the local culture could seem so cold. A thud and a squeal of laughter from Marilyn ends the ballad when the toilet seat collapses, leaving Philippe sitting in the dirt.

Even glum Cerilio manages a lopsided grin, revealing broken brown teeth.

"Bill, who is Cerilio?" I ask.

"He's my friend—sort of an aide-de-camp. We own a horse together. He showed me this trail four years ago when we rode through with Raul's father. Although he sleeps with the *arrieros*, he always stays close to me and the fire."

Philippe, recovered from his fall, passes the guitar to Raul, whose young falsetto voice reminds me of the high-pitched melancholy *huayños* I've heard at Indian festivals in the highland villages near Cusco. His broad flat nose and high cheekbones hint of Inca ancestry.

Darkness creeps closer around the dying fire, and Judy and I exchange tales of past campfires while the guitar is passed around, followed by Kate's rum bottle.

At eight o'clock we all retire to our tents. Kate, Tricia, and I sit cross-legged on our sleeping bags and arrange our belongings in our designated space.

"Nest-makers," says Kate.

"Homemakers, housewives, program directors—what are we?" Tricia asks, rubbing cream on her face. "But this trip is fabulous so far. God, I hope the horses aren't too wild. I wonder what Mike would think if he were here."

Mike—husbands—I'd almost forgotten them. "Do you think he'd like this trip?" I ask while trying to pull off my jeans in the confines of my corner.

"No, definitely not. He doesn't like poverty, dirt, or people peeing in the streets." Tricia screws the lid on the jar and tosses it in her pack. "Camping's not his thing. He likes nice hotels, warm beaches, good restaurants. . . ."

"This is no place for husbands," observes Kate with a smile. "As much as I love mine and like to travel with him, I'm glad he's not here." We both look at Kate, uncertain if we share her sentiments—or if we don't want to admit that we do.

"I don't know," Tricia begins slowly. "Mike wouldn't complain about the inconveniences and discomforts. He's very good about that."

"True," says Kate, lying back on her sleeping bag with her arms crossed under her head, "but you'd still be worrying all the time whether he was happy or not. You were trained that way, you know, to always feel responsible when things go wrong."

"That's typical female guilt," I respond.

"Well, that's one thing I like about this trip," Tricia says. "I'm not responsible for anyone but myself, so I have no guilt. Vacation is where you don't have to explain anything to anyone."

"You probably couldn't explain it if you wanted to," I observe. "Nothing on this trip has been the way I thought it would be."

"You're right," Kate says, sitting up. "If we don't know where we're going, when, or why we're going there, there's nothing to explain. So no responsibility—just guiltless ignorance."

"The best way to travel is to just let it happen," Tricia says with a sigh.

"That would drive Lars crazy," Kate replies. "He likes to make things happen his way. He needs to be in charge—to know what to expect, where we're going, how long it will take. He is an expert camper and would never put a tent in a dumb place like this—with rocks all over and sloping sideways. He doesn't need anyone to tell him how to make a fire or select a campsite."

"You'd probably tell him anyway," Tricia says, laughing.

"Probably, but I know he wouldn't burn the steak." She stares at the ceiling as if trying to remember what else was wrong with dinner.

"I really wanted Osvaldo to come on this trip," I say. "I thought it would be fun to share this kind of experience with him, but I'm actually glad he's not here." This is a startling revelation for me, and my two friends wait while I think about it.

"I have only traveled in South America on his terms. It's his culture, his language, his people. Things he takes for granted, I find fascinating—like the Indians. Argentines think being Indian is something to be ashamed of. I don't think Osvaldo thinks that, but I'm not sure."

"If Osvaldo were here," Tricia interjects, "he would dominate the entire trip. You would sit quietly and accept whatever he says. He's a dynamic person, and this is his territory."

"True. I wouldn't have my own conversations. I wouldn't draw my own conclusions. He would simply take over, and I would let him."

"Well, we get what we deserve," says Kate.

"Another curious thing," I add slowly, "is that I never knew his Latin culture was so appealing to me. Now that I see it from my point of view, I find I have a strange affinity for these people, this culture."

"That's probably why you married him," Tricia observes. "You fell for his culture as much as for him—perhaps because it's different." We think about that for a moment.

Kate sits suddenly upright on her sleeping bag. "I like not having to worry about anyone's welfare but my own. As wives and mothers, our lives revolve around concern for husband, kids—we even extend that to friends, jobs, and everyone we come in contact with. We're such fools. We do everything possible to make our families depend on us, and the more dependent they get, the more we don't like it."

"I guess we need to feel needed," Tricia says. "It's just that they seem to get more dependent as we get more independent. When we come home from this trip, we'll be so wildly independent, they won't know what to do with us."

We find that possibility hilarious.

I can hear Judy and Lauren in the tent next to us laughing also. Perhaps we should have done this when we were their age.

The three of us crawl out of the tent into the moonlit night—no need for a flashlight. With toilet paper stuffed into our pockets, we head for the bushes. I am sure our white gringa bottoms are luminescent in the moonlight, and I long to be dark and inconspicuous in this environment, like Cerilio.

Chapter Nine

THE LONG RIDE
TO CAMP AT SORAY

▼▼▼▼▼▼▼▼▼▼▼▼▼▼▼

I awake the next morning to the smell of coffee and the sound of Jaime singing a *huayno* about all the women who have left him.

Jose Maria Arguedas describes this typical Peruvian folk music in his book, *Ríos Profundos*:

> "Huayno is an indelible footprint the natives have engraved in their path of salvation and creation. Across generations, Huayno has recorded every moment of pain, joy, and terrible struggle . . . centuries later, natives still continue to find in this music the whole expression of their spirit."

Today's *huayno* mixes Andean folk with a modern beat from the coast. The melody sounds like a lament, but the rhythm is quick and repetitive.

Jaime sets the table in the cook tent with bowls for cereal, tin coffee cups, Pisac bread, and homemade marmalade.

We emerge from our tents, bundled in down parkas and sweat-pants over long underwear. I look longingly across the ravine to a spot where the sun shines on plowed fields and a small farm. A band of children from neighboring farms squat on their haunches by the cooking fire. Their clothes are bits of cloth sewn together. Their bare feet are red and swollen with the cold. Dark eyes in dirty, snot-smeared faces watch with fascination our morning ritual of sipping coffee and eating oatmeal. Philippe says not to give them any food. It encourages begging.

Jaime goes to talk to them in Quechua, and when Kate asks him if they are hungry, he tells her he will give them something to eat when we leave.

Judy and Lauren are still inside their tent. When Kate goes to investigate, she finds Lauren too sick to get up. She has been coughing and vomited during the night, and now, drowsy with a severe headache, isn't sure if she can continue. Judy and Kate consult Bill, who agrees that she has a severe case of altitude sickness, which will necessitate delaying our start.

Brad, a retired radiologist and the closest thing we have to a doctor, says, "If it is pulmonary edema, we will have to move her to a lower altitude."

The thought of evacuating one of our group before we've even begun plunges us into silent calculations. Could she ride back to Mollepata with an *arriero*? What then? Would she have to return to Cusco, which is higher than here? How would she get there? The truck that brought us has returned to Cusco by now. Kate, Judy, and Bill question Lauren inside her tent and decide to give her a dose of Kate's Diamox and let her rest in her sleeping bag until we are ready to depart.

"I thought Lauren hiked all over Switzerland last summer," Patti says. "She should be more fit than any of us."

"It's not a question of fitness," Brad replies. "Fitness and age have nothing to do with it."

"Strange, she didn't get sick in Cusco," Kate adds.

"That might be because we were there only one night, and she slept most of that afternoon," Judy replies.

"Even Edmund Hillary had to be evacuated in the Himalayas once," Kate reminds us, as we begin to dismantle our tent and pack up our saddlebags. Brad and Patti help Judy take her tent down, leaving Lauren to lie motionless in her sleeping bag.

Meanwhile, Jaime and Raul have packed up the food and taken down the crew and kitchen tents. Orange boxes lie open all about us. The lunch and first-aid boxes must be kept separate to go with us on the trail, while all the rest of the gear goes ahead with the *arrieros* and their pack animals. Philippe, Jaime, Bill, and Marilyn have spent hours trying to make the loads even for the burros. Philippe and Bill give directions. Marilyn tries putting all the pots and pans in one box, food in another, condiments and later dinners in another. The load is still uneven. Raul and Jaime unpack and repack the boxes, trying to stabilize the weight. At last the loads are approved by the *arrieros*. Lids are strapped on, and the *arrieros* load mules that stand about the campsite, waiting for their loads with hanging, blindfolded heads. Every morning we will go through this ritual, and every night the crew will open all fourteen boxes to find the salt, or a knife, or an onion.

Kate watches, controlling the urge to tell them how she could have done it better. "This would drive Lars crazy," she mutters, remembering camping trips with her husband.

Lauren is up and walking, her pale face framed by a mass of black, disheveled curls. "I feel much better than an hour ago," she says. "I'll be okay to ride."

"Listen to your body," Kate says. "It will tell you what you need. Drink water and tell us if you're not okay."

Lauren nods.

Cerilio introduces us to our horses. He and the other *arrieros* will walk the entire trip, while we ride their animals. They will help us on and off, tighten cinches, saddle and unsaddle their stock.

Tricia looks nervous and tries to remember how to get on. Cerilio holds the reins and gives her a leg up.

I wonder if these horses are accustomed to being mounted on the left. Bill says it doesn't matter, that the best side is the uphill side. This seems logical, since everything is uphill or downhill in Peru.

Brad pats a small, tired-looking, gray beast with a drooping head. "I tried to find one who was lame or nearly dead," he claims. "I interviewed them all, you know, and got accident reports and resumes. I think I'll call her Dulce Suave and hope she behaves accordingly—sweet and smooth."

My horse is a two-year-old male—frisky and stubborn, especially when separated from his mother. At least he's short, I think, as I settle down on the thick sheepskin that has been thrown over a wooden frame to make a saddle.

During the confusion of loading pack animals and adjusting cinches and stirrups, one of the *arrieros* takes off with Brad, Pat, and Don. Bill is furious and shouts at them in English and in Spanish to come back. Brad looks back helplessly over his shoulder and disappears into the brush.

Seeing me mounted, Bill asks me to go after them. I kick my horse, loosen the reins, and lean forward in the saddle. No response. On inspecting the bridle, I see that the reins are tied to a rope around the horse's nose. With no bit in his mouth, I realize I have little influence on his behavior. I lean forward again, grip hard with my knees—do all the things a rider would do on a normal horse to make him go—but instead of moving forward, we go backwards. Then we make a little circle, run up the hill and back down.

Bill realizes I have no control over my horse. He yells at Cerilio to stop the riders, but Cerilio is on foot, and they are away before he can catch up.

"We'll catch up to them along the way," Cerilio says with a shrug.

Antonín, with his head wrapped in a clean bandage, leads our procession: eleven riders, four *arrieros* on foot, and two pack animals with lunch and first aid. My horse falls obediently into line in front of his mother.

Brilliant red bushes with flowers like Indian paintbrush embrace us in a tangle of crimson branches as our horses puff and pant up a steep rocky trail, zigzagging ever higher into the mountains until we reach a plateau covered with dense clumps of *ichu*—the tough grass that grows only above ten thousand feet. When my horse jerks his head down to grab a bite of this nourishing treat, the rough rawhide reins rip the skin off my hands. I make a mental note to get gloves out of my pack tonight.

Antonín tells me that he owns my horse and the two in front (ridden by Kate and Lauren), and that the one behind (ridden by Judy) is my horse's mother. These horses cannot be separated. Later, when I try to ride ahead with Kate and Tricia, Antonín takes my reins and puts me back where I belong. I wonder if we will have to remain in this order the entire trip.

Antonín's son, Mario, walks behind me. His belongings are wrapped in a poncho and slung across his shoulder, leaving his arms free to play the *quena* (Andean flute). He wears a red Budweiser cap and promises he will take care of me if I give him cigarettes, candy, a cigarette lighter, my sweatpants, and anything else I don't want.

The trail steepens, becomes rockier, and finally is so steep that Antonín signals us to get off and lead our horses to the top, where we must cross a slope that is just a few degrees less than vertical. A slide of loose shale has swept a portion of the trail off the mountainside. I hesitate, trusting my horse's four feet more than my two. Years of riding in rugged terrain with my father and later with my children has taught me that horses don't like to fall down any more than we do, and that more often than not, they can carry us safely over seemingly impossible trails.

Reluctantly, I dismount, sending a few loose rocks over the edge. I can't hear where they land. I can hear the steady roar of a river three thousand feet below. I look ahead and see Cerilio holding Tricia's hand and leading her horse. That's good, I think, as I walk carefully along a path that slopes menacingly away toward the canyon. My little horse follows obediently, and I hold the reins tightly—since they're the only thing I have to hold onto.

When we reach the other side of the slide and remount (on the uphill side), Bill tells us about a psychiatrist from New York who crawled on his stomach over this part of the trail last year. Tricia looks at Bill with tight lips and cold, green eyes.

Antonín leads us single file upward, out of the brush and onto an open slope where, at last, I see a snow-covered mountain looming above misty clouds. It begins to rain, and we pull parkas and rain ponchos out of our saddlebags. I fumble for my camera, trying to capture the gray, glacial splendor of that brooding peak without dropping reins or gloves or getting tangled in a billowing poncho.

We stop for a quick lunch in a rock-strewn meadow.

"I wonder where the others are," Bill says to no one in particular. "They won't have any lunch." He asks Cerilio if the *arriero* they are with will know where to stop and make camp.

"*Pues, no sé, Señor Bill.* (I don't know)," Cerilio replies.

"I Don't Know" could be the title of a new *huayno*, I think.

"*I don't know where we are going . . . I don't know how far . . . don't know how difficult the terrain . . . don't know if it will snow or rain . . . I don't know where our friends have gone or if they're lost. . . .*"

Without speaking Spanish, Brad, Pat, and Don can't ask the bad *arriero* who rode off with them where they are or how far it is to where they're going.

We mount our horses and continue in a cold drizzle. On several occasions, the *arrieros* signal us to dismount and lead our horses over some part of the trail they deem too difficult or dangerous to ride. I wonder who makes these decisions—Bill or Antonín. I think the dangers of getting on and off outweigh the dangers of the terrain. This constant stopping gives my horse the opportunity to mill about and bite and kick the others. It makes me nervous. However, I don't know what lies ahead, so I have to obey the orders that are passed back to me.

After one of these stops on the crest of a gentle hill by a shallow ravine, I watch Kate get back on her horse. She puts one foot in the stirrup, gathers up the reins, and swings the other leg up—but not quite over—her saddlebag which lies across the horse's rump. As she tries again to swing her leg over the saddlebag, her horse begins to walk forward and then to trot downhill in a jerky gait. Kate, struggling now to hang on to the saddle, loosens the reins, and the horse bolts forward, throwing her to the side of the trail, where she lands on the bank of the ravine. There is no *arriero* to grab the reins, and no one ahead looks back.

Judy, Lauren, and I stop our horses, expecting Kate to sit up, swear at the goddamn horse, and get back on. She doesn't move.

I shout to the others ahead, "Stop! Kate has fallen!" I get off and run to where she lies in a bed of leaves and twigs. Bill and the riders ahead don't hear my shouts. They continue along the trail until the riderless horse gallops into their midst.

Judy kneels down with me next to Kate, who lies curled up and motionless. I can't believe she is hurt—not Kate, not here, not from a stupid fall off a horse.

"It's my back, I think. I can't move." She winces with pain.

Bill and the others have left their horses with the *arrieros* and gather in a helpless group around our fallen comrade. We consider our options.

It is a two- or three-day ride to the nearest town in either direction, and there is no telephone in either place. From Mollepata, it's a long truck ride back to Cusco. I have no idea how you get to Cusco from the other end of our six-day ride—unless it's the train we take to Machu Picchu. There are no rescue facilities in Peru.

Bill asks Judy: How badly is she hurt? How did it happen? Can she get up? Can she go on? And Marilyn discusses various evacuation strategies.

Feeling inadequate, ignorant, and somewhat to blame for her injuries, I watch Judy kneel over Kate and embrace her the way nurses turn patients over in a hospital bed. With Kate giving instructions and Judy gently maneuvering, Kate struggles to an upright position.

"Just a moment . . . I'll be all right," she says. "I have no choice, do I?"

Bill looks like he wants to put his arms around her but doesn't dare touch her.

In a few minutes, with Judy's assistance, Kate stands up, walks a bit, looks at the horse that threw her, and decides to ride a different one. With Cerilio's help, she gets on Bill's horse, and Cerilio takes the reins, leading the horse forward while watching Kate's expression at every step.

Bill tells me it could be dark before we reach camp. Later that afternoon, riding solemnly across a rock-strewn field with no vegetation, I hunch over my horse and shiver under a dripping rain poncho, aware of my own vulnerability in this barren and remote place. Part of me loves the wild, desolate panorama of brooding peaks lurking above and around in a gray mist, and part of me hates the cold, incessant rain, numb fingers, hunger, exhaustion, and this interminable trail where the only sound is the sharp click of horses' hooves on cold stones. We ride beneath great gray, headless mountains, insignificant as ants, searching for the sight of our friends with the errant *arriero*, hoping to see a campsite. At last we discern our tents far ahead, and I thank God and the *arrieros* that we don't have to put them up ourselves.

Brad, Patti, and Don greet us with much relief. "Wait 'til you hear what happened to us," Patti says.

"Later," Bill replies. "We've got to get Kate inside the crew tent."

Chapter Ten

THE CAMP BENEATH SORAY

▼▼▼▼▼▼▼▼▼▼▼▼▼▼▼

Bill and Brad, with the help of Cerilio, ease Kate off her horse, bundle her in sleeping bags, and help her lie down in our tent. Brad examines her, gently poking and pressing up and down her spine.

"You could have bruised a vertebra," he tells her. "It might even be fractured—sure hope not, because movement will be painful."

"She's pretty sore all over," he tells us. "Maybe has a cracked pelvis."

"She's in shock," Judy says as Kate shivers inside her cocoon of down bags and ponchos.

Tricia brings the rum bottle, and Bill fetches codeine from a first-aid box. Kate, being a nurse, has a good supply of medicines for all sorts of emergencies. I am sure her intention was to administer them to someone other than herself.

While trying to make the tent as comfortable as possible, Tricia and I discuss the possibilities of an injured back. What if it is a cracked pelvis? We know so little. As with everything else, we'll just have to take each event as it happens. Tricia and I know that Kate the nurse will imagine the worst possibilities—ruptured spleen, crushed kidney, things we know nothing about.

Dusk fades quickly, and it's dark by six o'clock. We gather by the fire, our tin cups filled with pisco and Tang.

"Why did you guys ride off and leave us?" Bill finally asks Brad.

"We had little to say in the matter. When you told the four of us to go ahead, Miguel grabbed Don's horse's reins and pulled him up the hill. The guy literally ran up that hill. Our horses just followed at the same pace."

"We kept asking him where we were going," Don adds. "How far? Where are the rest? All he ever said was, '*Sí*.' There was no way we could find out what was going on. We couldn't communicate."

"I've never used that *arriero* before," Bill says. "I gave him hell for leading you off like that."

"I was really scared," Pat admits. "We kept looking back for you—not a sign. We had no idea if we were going in the right direction. He wouldn't even stop and wait for you for lunch. We were starved. Don had only a banana."

Don describes their one stop. "There was a stone hut in that bleak rocky meadow. Miguel went inside, and I thought maybe he lived there."

"I thought we had arrived at our campsite," Pat interrupts.

"It was cold, filthy, and too exposed to be a campsite," Don continues. "I wondered if we were being abducted at that point."

Bill laughs, and Pat says, "Anyway, Miguel seemed to know the lady who lived there. She gave us a bowl of soup that we passed around. It was lumpy, but warm. Guinea pigs ran all over, and the fireplace where they cook had no chimney, so smoke and ashes were all over."

"Sounds like a great experience," Judy says.

"Well, we were sure happy when Cerilio showed up and led us to the right camp," Pat says.

Brad looks puzzled. "I wonder how he knew where we were."

A bundled figure emerges from the crew tent and shuffles over to the fire with outstretched cup.

"I knew she wouldn't miss the cocktail hour," Tricia says. "Thank God you're up and alive."

"I'm not sure I am," Kate answers, smiling meekly.

After dinner, we insert Kate carefully into her sleeping bag. Sleep will not come easily at thirteen thousand feet on a bed of rocks. More codeine and rum are prescribed. Tricia and I return to the fire to join Judy and Lauren. Raul sits squarely in front of Lauren, his guitar resting on his knees. He sings to her with his eyes half closed.

"*Te gusta?* (You like it?)" he asks, lips curving slowly into a smile.

"Oh yes, sing another," she begs.

"Sing something happy," Judy suggests.

"*Para tí*, anything," Raul replies. After more songs and more rum, Raul comes and sits on a log next to me, and we talk in Spanish about the day's events. He tells me that Kate wouldn't let Cerilio hold her horse while she was getting on.

"Cerilio was up ahead," I reply. "He probably didn't know she got off."

"She should have called him," Raul says. He thinks Kate was being too proud for her own good, and that Lauren is very pretty. I tell him that Kate is proud—that all of us like to do things for ourselves, and that he should get to know Judy, as she speaks Spanish.

Taking my advice, Raul gets up and goes and sits next to her, puts his arm around her and kisses her on the cheek. "Hey, what's this?" she asks, looking at him and then at me.

"*Tu eras mi amor.* (You are my love)," he declares with a melodic giggle.

WE ARE ALL IN OUR TENTS WHEN a soft but steady rain begins to fall. I think Kate will probably sleep sounder than any of us with the help of her rum and codeine, but she will be stiff in the morning.

It rains all night. During one fierce downpour, I lie awake thinking about the four twenty-thousand-foot peaks above us—about the streams fed by their receding glaciers that rush down their sides and cause flash floods that have wiped out entire villages. The relentless sound of the rain and the closeness of the tent send my imagination soaring to northern Peru, where a hanging glacier let loose and crashed down the valley causing monumental mudslides that buried a town of thirty thousand people who were never found.

Suddenly, as if answering my wild premonitions, there's a crash and a frightened squeal from outside the tent. I sit upright, only to find the tent has caved in on my side. Cerilio is shouting outside the door. Neither Tricia nor I can find our flashlights. I know it wasn't a glacier because we're still alive. I unzip the door and peer into the night, expecting at least a small avalanche. Cerilio, who was sleeping under the overhang of our tent, explains that the water build up on the roof was too heavy for the supports. When it gave way, all the water dumped on him. Poor Cerilio. He drags his wet poncho off to the crew tent, where Bill, Raul, and Jaime are sleeping. The rest of the *arrieros* have disappeared to seek their own kind of shelter. Kate never wakes up. We check that she is still breathing.

At seven in the morning, I zip open the front tent flap and look up to a clear sky. The only sound I hear is the contented munching of three horses grazing in a pasture a few feet in front of me. Having arrived late the night before, I wonder what lies up the trail leading out of our camp, so I pull on my boots, grab my camera, and walk up to a wide meadow, hushed and empty in the pale light of dawn.

Salcantay is wholly visible and dominates the scene with its great white presence, rising above the earth and filling the western sky—waiting, as it has done forever, to greet the sun's first rays of light. We wait together.

Directly to my left, Humantay, almost as high as Salcantay, pierces the sky with its icy, wind-sculpted pinnacles. I sit on a rock

Salcantay, 20,574 ft., before dawn

Humantay, 17,986 ft at dawn

and watch the sun illuminate its uppermost spires. One by one they light up and sparkle in the pale sky like a crown atop a sleeping giant. I want to photograph everything, but how can I capture the shades of light, the enormity of the mountains, the solitude of the meadow?

I return to a bustling campsite. Tent covers, tarps, and sleeping bags are festooned about the trees and bushes. The cooks are busy with the eternal search in the orange boxes for breakfast ingredients, and everyone else is packing his saddle bag in preparation for today's long ride. All of this activity is closely observed by three Indian children and their father, who all squat motionless on the periphery of our camp. Our pile of food and equipment must seem like an incredible excess to them.

Brad comes toward us, walking slowly from the direction of the latrine. He is holding his side, trying not to laugh, and he looks pained and puzzled. His pants are wet up to his waist.

"What happened to you?" Pat asks, emerging from their tent.

"You won't believe this," he replies. "I was seated comfortably on the toilet seat, gazing up at the glaciers," he points and winces, "and I fell off."

"You fell off? Off the seat?"

"Well, it's my fault, I guess. I set it up on a rather precarious ridge, and while I was sitting there, I leaned back, and the seat tilted, and I fell backwards down the bank, about twelve feet, into the river!"

"Are you hurt?" Pat asks, touching his side.

"I think my ribs are bruised—maybe broken. Also, tumbling down over all those rocks with my pants tangled up around my ankles . . ."

What ignominious injuries, I think. One falls off her horse and another falls off the john. What next?

Kate is up and walking, testing how much she can move and contemplating what to eat and how many painkillers will get her through today. She and Brad discuss their injuries and concerns for the day's trip.

How far are we riding?

Bill doesn't know how far in miles.

How long will it take?

That depends on how often we stop, what happens along the way, how fast the animals move. . . .

How steep will it be?

Pretty steep.

As usual, there are few answers. Kate, Pat, and Brad want more specific details, but Bill seems reluctant to commit to anything specific. To most of us, it doesn't matter. To Brad and Kate, it does.

Chapter Eleven

SALCANTAY

▼▼▼▼▼▼▼▼▼▼▼▼▼▼▼

The usual packing, unpacking, loading, and redistributing loads on mules, plus tending to the wounded, delays our start to midmorning. At last, we head up the trail on frisky horses. When we reach the wide open meadow, Brad rides up next to me, and my horse suddenly whips his head around and bites Brad's horse in the neck. When I pull my horse's head back with the reins, he kicks the horse behind us. Then he takes off after Brad's horse, jumping around until he falls on all four knees. I feel like a bronc rider in a rodeo, except instead of raising one hand in the air, I hang on to the pommel.

Antonín and Mario come running to grab my reins, which frightens the horse even more. He gallops across the meadow with me barely hanging on and pulling on the reins while wondering if I'll be the next casualty.

At last we run out of meadow, and the horse stops. Bill cheers. Brad is horrified. From then on, the other riders keep their distance.

Back in formation, our horses slip and stumble, pant and strain, as we climb up the steep, rocky trail. Riders lean forward in the saddle and try not to look down or back. I am looking ahead,

Rugged, rocky trail around

And up

concentrating on how I'll get around the next rock, or over a slick granite slab, and wondering if the trail can possibly go up such a steep incline. Like the thread in an ancient textile, our trail winds and loops, disappears and emerges, weaving its way in switchbacks up the mountainside.

I look high into the sky, trying to calculate how far it is to the top of the pass, and I see two condors, the largest flying birds on earth, cruising above twenty thousand feet—so effortless their mode of travel, so laborious ours. What are they thinking when they look down on a little train of earthlings crawling snail-like over this hostile terrain?

At last we reach a small, windy plateau, protected on one side by a long mound of ground-up granite, the remains of a lateral moraine left by a long-ago glacier. It is so neatly packed that it could have been deposited there yesterday by a bulldozer. Boulders the size of small houses, also left behind by the glacier, are scattered about the area, and we gather between them, seeking protection from the wind. Temperatures vary uncontrollably as clouds steal the warmth from the sun and send us digging in our packs for vests and parkas. After a quick snow flurry, the sun returns. It's hot again, so we take off one layer of clothing and put it back in our packs.

The *arrieros* huddle together smoking and watching their stock. They tell me it is better to smoke than to eat at this altitude. I look at their bare brown feet in rubber sandals made from tire retreads just like the ones Kate bought in the Pisac market. They are wet and muddy from crossing glacial streams, and I wonder if they feel cold or numb or anything. . . .

Bill reminds us of our late start and the necessity to get over the pass and down to camp before dark, so after a brief stop, we're back in the saddle and climbing a thousand feet higher. I begin to notice little stone cairns—*apachetas*—along the side of the trail.

These signify our arrival at the top of the pass, just short of sixteen thousand feet.

Everyone dismounts, hands their reins to an *arriero*, and scrambles over rocks and around boulders to look at Salcantay. For a moment, the enormous white mountain fills the sky. Then it vanishes behind flowing clouds that drift over the sharp crags, deep crevasses, and shining snow fields.

I am desperate to get as close as I can to this grand spectacle, but it is rough going over the giant rocks that the glacier has piled up over the centuries. Just as I find the perfect rock to sit on and peer over the edge, I hear a low rumble and then a thunderous crash. A segment of the glacier has broken off and tumbles in a shower of sparkling snow and ice into the cold blue chasm below.

I have never seen anything so big, so powerful, or so magnificent. Salcantay, "Wild One," lives up to its name, enticing me to enjoy its serenity, yet warning me to beware its fury.

I walk carefully back over the rocks to my horse, calm and confident that I have witnessed a scene that will stay with me forever.

Salcantay at my feet

Glacier breaking away

I know that the importance of this moment will manifest itself in many unexpected ways far from this windy pass.

With the confidence of a crusader who has captured the Holy Grail, I mount my horse and begin the arduous descent into the upper Amazon watershed.

THIS STEEP ROCKY ROAD WAS ONCE the pride of Inca road builders, and I can see remnants of ancient interlocking blocks and carefully laid steps that time and travelers have reduced to a crumbling hazard and a nuisance.

Called *Capac Nan*, "Beautiful Road," this road was part of a magnificent highway system that crisscrossed Peru from the coast through the Andes and all the way from Ecuador to Chile and Northern Argentina. For thousands of miles (fourteen thousand charted to date), it plunged through deep jungles, traversed rolling uplands, wound around narrow ledges, and crossed a thousand delicate vine bridges that hung precariously over white frothy rivers.

Where possible, these roads were perfectly straight, never deviating for towns or private property. (There was no private property in Inca times.) Up and down these meticulously maintained paths, the *chasquis* (post runners) could travel 150 miles in a day. They carried messages from Lima to Cusco in three days. It took the Spaniards thirteen days to do the same on horseback.

Tambos, or resting places, were strategically placed at the end of a day's journey, where another *chasqui* would be waiting to relay the message. The *tambos* were maintained and supplied by the government, so that a tired *chasqui* always had a good meal, fresh clothes, and shelter for the night.

Many of the Inca roads in the mountains are still used today, but they are not maintained as they were then, and the traffic no longer consists of barefoot runners.

For three decades, The Inca, as the ruler of the empire was known, administered this vast realm, keeping in touch with his subjects through this vital communication system. Father Bernabe Cobo wrote in his *History of the Inca Empire*, "If The Inca felt like having something especially delicious that needed to be brought from far away, such as fresh fish from the sea while he was in Cusco, his order was acted upon with such speed that, although the city was over seventy leagues from the sea, the fish was brought to him very fresh in less than two days."

Pizarro called the Inca road "a thing worthy of being seen." He was so impressed that he wrote, "Such beautiful roads could not, in truth, be found anywhere in Christendom," and Bernabe Cobo said, "Considering the lack of equipment and tools, these roads were magnificent constructions, which could be compared favorably with the most superb roads of the Romans."

BY NOW THE PACK ANIMALS and most of the *arrieros* are far ahead. Once again, Bill urges us to keep moving, as night will fall suddenly on the other side of the mountain.

Going downhill is as arduous mentally as going up is physically. The horses pick their way over loose, slippery rocks, causing their riders to lurch forward and backward in their saddles, swaying from side to side while taking parkas off and then putting them back on again. I wonder how Kate is feeling. Her spine must be twisting and turning at each downhill plunge of her horse's tired legs. On one switchback, I'm able to look back and see her walking. Cerilio is leading her horse.

Tired of the uneven gait, the constant lurching forward, backward, and sideways, I get off and lead my horse for a while. I want to look back at Salcantay, now that the rose and amber rays of sunset are beginning to wash over its smooth steep shoulders. I want to look back but am afraid I'll trip, so after a few stumbles and wading through a stream, I get back on my horse and let him do the stumbling. The *arrieros* walk through the milky-white water of glacial streams without a wince. I can feel the mountain's presence above and behind me all the way down the trail to camp.

It is much farther and longer than I anticipated, and hikers and riders are still strung out along the trail behind me when Tricia, I, and a few others arrive at dusk. The *arrieros* greet us, take our reins, and pull off the heavy saddlebags. Tricia and I immediately set out in search of a tent site that won't be too rocky, too uneven, or too hard, and as close as possible to the cook tent. It's getting late, and the sun has already disappeared behind the mountains. We have to make a decision. Kicking cow turds right and left, we clear the best place we can find. Judy and Lauren have their tent up first, so they come to help us. We toss our packs inside, find soap, shampoo, and a towel, and hurry over to the river where the other girls are bathing.

Straddling a small stream on my knees, I dunk my head in the icy water, rub half a bottle of biodegradable shampoo on my head, dunk again, and come up cold and not dripping. My hair is a frozen helmet.

I walk back to the campsite listening to the sharp *snap, click, crack* of cinches and straps being undone as the *arrieros* unpack the mules and send them off to graze with the familiar cry, *"Mula!"*

Kate, having walked instead of ridden down the pass, arrives when it's almost dark. She crawls into the tent and looks at the pile of sleeping bags.

"How are you?" Tricia and I both ask at once.

"Glad to be here, I guess," she answers. "I don't know why the hell Bill never told me how far we had to go. Every time I asked him or one of the *arrieros*, they always said, '*Un poco más, señora . . .*' Shit, if I'd known it was this far, I wouldn't have walked so much. I would have taken more codeine."

"Maybe they were afraid to tell you," Tricia suggests.

"Or they weren't really sure themselves," I wonder aloud.

Kate unzips her saddlebag and pulls out a thick black-and-brown alpaca sweater and a puffy red down parka. Tricia and I have already rolled out her sleeping bag on two Ensolite pads plus a poncho donated by Jaime.

"This is a lousy campsite, worse than the last one," she complains.

"We tried to get the rocks and manure out before we set up the tent," Tricia says.

"I know, but it's still a bad site. It's sloping, and there are grassier places above and below us." Kate tries to get up from a sitting position by rolling over onto all fours. "I want a real bed," she moans. "Where's the toilet paper?"

I hand it to her as she backs out of the tent and finally stands upright.

Tricia and I know that nothing will be right until we reach the Machu Picchu Hotel. I try to empathize with her pain and fatigue, but I can't. Exhausted and overwhelmed by all the emotions and experiences of the day, I can't find room for another feeling. Poor Kate. She is alone in her private hell.

It is dark when we assemble around the campfire. Hyper-exhilarated by a day filled with physical and personal challenges, the drama of scenery beyond all expectations, and the fact that we are here in this place, we celebrate with long-awaited tin cups of pisco. Each of us has experienced a mixture of wonder and pride in the knowledge that we have conquered the wilderness and made its wild beauty part of ourselves forever.

"I'm so glad I'm here," Tricia announces, raising her cup.

"Me too," Don adds. "Never in my life will there be another trip like this."

"A toast for Dulce Suave, finest horse in the Andes," Brad says, touching his cup to Pat's. They smile affectionately at one another.

I look through the smoke at Kate. Wearing a droopy, gray poncho, she looks like a female *arriero*. The mixture of codeine and pisco has given her the same vacant stare as a lifetime of chewing coca leaves. Jaime fills her cup and lights a sparkle in her eyes. She thanks him, and her weathered face softens in relaxed contentment.

We crowd as close to the fire as we dare, enveloped in smoke and the strong scent of cedar.

Perched rather precariously on a rock, I dig into the spicy beef *saltado* served on a cold tin plate, warming my hands at the fire between mouthfuls. Everything tastes good, feels good, smells good, except that I can't get close enough to the fire without getting in it.

In the flickering shadows that play upon the slope beyond, I can barely see the shapes of six *arrieros* who seem to grow out of the dark earth like mushrooms under their ponchos. Black shapeless hats cover sweat-flattened hair and shade their faces. The dark pupils in their eyes are the only things that move. Bill goes to give them cigarettes and invites them to come share the warmth of the fire. Their brown weathered hands extend from beneath tattered ponchos and are held motionless above the flames. When Bill makes them laugh, crooked yellow teeth are exposed to the glow of the fire.

It is cold tonight—below freezing. The *arrieros* will sleep under their ponchos next to the fire. Kate has rewarded Cerilio's devotion by "lending" him an alpaca sweater similar to the one she wears. As I shiver in my sleeping bag, waiting for sleep to rest a taut but weary body, I think of the events of the day. "*It was the best of times, it was the worst of times.*"

I cannot go to sleep. I forgot to unroll my bag before dinner so the down would fluff up. I put on sweatpants and a sweatshirt over my long underwear, but this added bulk probably only makes things worse. I can't stop shivering. Is it fatigue? Hypothermia? Kate is drugged again, so I can't ask her. I can't stop shaking, which makes me even more tired.

Far away in that dark other world of night, I hear the crash and thunder of frozen snow sliding off some distant glacier. Salcantay reminds me once again that nature is both violence and peace, and I am comforted by a feeling of permanence. Salcantay will always be there. No one can take it away.

Just before dawn, which should be the coldest hour of the day, I find myself warm and content, lying very close to Tricia. The warmth that emanates from her sleeping bag finally puts me to sleep. When I tell her this later, she laughs. "I'm glad you're enjoying my hot flashes. Usually they keep me awake. At least they're good for something, if they put you to sleep."

At last the sun has reached the cook tent. Jaime is making coffee and singing a new *huayño*.

I crawl out of our tent with toilet paper in my pocket and a frozen wash rag. The *arrieros* are out and about, looking for horses, chasing off dogs from a farmhouse nearby, and gathering firewood. I climb higher up the trail toward a stream I remember crossing yesterday. I'm hoping to reach the spot where the sun has drawn a line across the slope above our camp. On the way, I find a rock the size of a small hotel and disappear behind it. When I emerge to continue up to the stream, I notice a thick fog moving up the valley from the Amazon watershed. Our campsite sits just above the clouds.

At last I reach the stream, but the warmth of the sun is still a long ways off. A few minutes later, hair combed and face washed in icy water, I'm ready for breakfast.

But when I stand up to head back to camp, I find it has been obliterated by the fog. No matter, I think, I only need to walk downhill. However, I am lost immediately in a thick cloud. I keep walking straight ahead—but am I really walking straight? There is no trail to follow. Might I have veered a bit to the right, which is also down? If so, I would be heading for some cliffs.

I hesitate. The ground seems level for as far as I can see, but this is only about one foot. I'm not sure which way is up or down. I continue in what I hope is the right direction, but see no familiar landmark, hear no sounds of horses in the fog.

I will not succumb to this feeling of helpless panic that is making my heart beat faster. Should I wait right here until the fog clears? No, who knows how long this fog will last? Maybe all day. All the horses will be saddled, the tents struck, and I'll still be lost. I'm probably only a few hundred yards from camp, but I can't hear Jaime singing, and no one even knows I'm out here.

I veer to the left and walk rapidly away from where I think the cliffs might be. This must be down. I must be going toward camp. For the first time on this trip, I'm truly frightened. The shadow of a large rock takes shape in front of me. Have I been here before? The shape of a man comes out from behind it, and I pray it will be someone from our group, someone familiar, someone who will save me and not think I'm stupid. The figure stands still and looks in my direction.

There is nothing to do but to walk towards him. It's Raul.

"*Señora Eddy, que haces aqui? Estas perdida?* (What are you doing here? Are you lost?)"

He must see the relief in my face, the joy of finding a friend in the middle of a cloud. He walks quickly to where I am standing and puts strong young arms around me. He doesn't ask me how I got here, if I were frightened, or why didn't I know better than to wander so far from camp. With a reassuring hug, he tells me the fog has already blown beyond the camp, and I follow him into the sunlight and the smell of bacon cooking.

Clouds recede from camp

Chapter Twelve

FROM ICHU GRASS
TO ORCHIDS

▼▼▼▼▼▼▼▼▼▼▼▼▼

By ten o'clock, our wash rags have thawed, ice has melted in the stream, tents are struck, pack animals are loaded, and horses (not as frisky as yesterday) are saddled. Kate communicates by sign language to Cerilio that she will walk with Judy, Tricia, and Don. They leave half an hour ahead of us.

The rest of us follow Antonín over a tangle of cow paths that crisscross the open slope below our camp. Before the trail descends into the upper Amazon jungle, I take a last glance back at Humantay, shining now in full sunlit splendor high above us. No wonder the Incas called their highest mountains *Apu* (God) and believed that mountain spirits watched over them, protecting their land and livestock. Such a sight would make me a believer.

Salcantay and the snowy peaks of the Andes recede into memory as we disappear one by one into a tunnel of spiny bushes with yellow flowers all entangled in vines of brilliant red and orange blossoms. Strange tropical plants appear with more regularity.

"Look!" Pat exclaims, pointing at a tangle of bromeliads clinging to a thorny tree.

When we pass a mass of small, white orchids, also growing out of a tree, Pat says, "Those are epiphytes, orchids that live on another tree. I think the yellow ones over there," she says, pointing up the hill from us, "are *oncidium scansor*."

Pat rides along ahead of me, naming each species of orchid and bromeliad as we encounter them.

Four hours pass, and we're still descending. Along the way, I notice little trails that disappear into the undergrowth above and below me, and occasionally I catch a glimpse of a fence, a lean-to, an abandoned clearing. *Who lives here?* I wonder.

Abruptly, the vegetation ends. It appears to have been ripped from its roots by a massive rockslide that has tumbled down from somewhere high above us, carrying with it a large swath of tropical foliage, a few shacks, and our trail. We dismount to assess the situation.

Antonín tells me it happened a month ago during the rainy season. I look above and below and try to imagine the catastrophic proportions of such a slide. Were there witnesses? Victims? We lead our horses across a faint trail of loose rocks, stumps, and shattered vines.

On the other side, the trail continues downward, just as it has all morning. Directly across the canyon on a perpendicular slope three thousand feet above the river, plots of land cultivated in vertical rows appear to hang like small brown-and-russet carpets.

"What do you suppose is growing over there?" I ask Bill, who rides in front of me.

"Beats me. It must be something special, because you'd have to have a ladder or be roped to something to get in there and plant or harvest it. If we were in California, I'd say it was marijuana," he says with a chuckle.

"If that side's as steep as this one," I say, "one misstep and you'd fall to the bottom of the canyon. They must work lying on their stomachs."

We continue downward for another hour when, at last, the trail levels off, and we converge on a small green pampa, where we meet a family with their livestock. Bill tells us we will be meeting more farmers transporting their goods to market, as we descend in the direction of Santa Teresa—our ultimate destination.

Cows and children watch us with equal curiosity as we dismount, loosen cinches, and leave our horses to wander while we stretch stiff legs and disappear behind available trees.

I spy Kate's bright purple shirt and orange backpack down the trail by a stream, where she, Tricia, Don, and Judy have been waiting for us for about an hour. After admiring the band of exotic flowers that encircle Kate's tribal hat, I ask how she is.

"It still hurts, mostly when I bend over. I'm really looking forward to the hot spring at the end of the day," she says.

"Well, how was it?" Bill asks them as he opens the lunch crate and hands us each an orange.

"Longer than we expected," Tricia answers. "At first, we weren't sure which way to go. There were so many little paths that led nowhere. We had to cross lots of streams and marshes—things you guys just ride over."

"At least we knew we had to go down," Don adds. "At first, we could hear you behind us, but after a while, nothing. There was no definite trail, and we didn't know if there were little streams or serious rivers ahead."

"It was fun, though," Judy says. "Kind of like being explorers."

"You know Kate's imagination," Tricia says, looking at me and smiling. "She was sure we were in the wrong canyon and would never see any of you again."

"And that we were headed for some unknown Amazonian village for the rest of our lives," Judy adds.

Being lost hadn't occurred to me, but of course, Antonín was leading us.

Kate grimaces, changes position on her rock, and says, "I don't like walking for hours in this wild country where you never see a living soul, and you have no idea where you're going."

"The hot spring will be a great relief," Tricia says.

"What about that slide?" Don asks. "That must have been a horrendous event!"

"We saw lots of smaller ones," Kate adds. "They must be happening all the time."

We decide to delay lunch until we reach the hot spring. After various attempts to ascertain distance, time, and terrain, Kate and the walkers decide to follow the pack train and arrive ahead of us so they can enjoy the hot mineral baths before us.

Back in the saddle, we slip and slide down a muddy embankment only to dismount again at a wide stream. A fragile-looking bridge of logs and loose planks held together by vines and bits of stringy rope has been recently constructed.

Crossing a delicate bridge

Antonín leads his horse across. Brad is next. He starts across the bridge, leading Dulce Suave, who decides she doesn't like it, bolts, and runs in the opposite direction, leaving Brad in the middle of the bridge, where he manages to regain his balance and return to the bank. Cerilio and Bill coax the frightened horse out of the bushes and lead her across, with Brad following. Pat's horse crosses without incident, followed by the rest of us.

For the next three hours, I ride along, thinking the hot spring will be just around the corner. Bill is far ahead, Cerilio too far back to ask.

At last, the trail levels, and we arrive at an open field. A few stone and adobe houses, children, and about twenty dogs give the sense of a village. The hikers are lying in the grass, exhausted. Are we there? No.

"We never dreamed it would be this far." Tricia sighs. "If I'd known, I would have gotten back on the horse at the last stop."

Judy, lying on her back with arms outstretched, opens one eye and says, "The pack train and our horses passed us a long time ago. Now we have to walk."

Bill offers his horse, but no one wants to get up off the grass. "It's just at the bottom of this hill," he says, hoping to console them. "I forgot there was so much uphill after the last stop. I promise, it's all down from here."

Fifteen switchbacks later, we drop into a narrow canyon. The trail follows a river and passes a hot spring, which oozes out of copper-colored cliffs onto the muddy trail. I slog past the site, concentrating on crossing a narrow vine bridge over the turbulent Santa Teresa River. *Was that little ooze I just rode by the hot spring?* I wonder.

Cerilio tells us that since Bill last visited this much-anticipated campsite, someone has cut all the trees down and left them rotting on the ground. Reluctant *arrieros* and exhausted campers will have to clear the area, dragging the branches out of the way, before we can unload the mules, erect tents, and unpack. Mosquitoes, no-see-ums, and vicious black flies attack.

Soon the area is campable. Jaime helps me erect our tent in the flattest place I can find with a view of the river.

Kate hates it. It slopes, it's lumpy, it's too hot, and the door faces the wrong way. She crawls inside, throws herself on her saddlebag, and collapses in tears.

"Why does the crew tent always get the only flat ground at every camp?" she complains. "When will I ever get to sleep in a bed again?"

Tricia comes in and tries to console our fallen comrade. "Let's go find the hot spring," she suggests.

"There isn't any goddamn hot spring," Kate replies. "Everyone lies to us. Didn't you see that little trickle on the trail? How am I supposed to sit in that?"

"It's useless," Tricia says, shrugging her shoulders. "Kate just needs to cry."

We leave her alone in the tent and carry our towels, shampoo, and clean underwear up the trail.

The hot mud feels good on tired feet. Judy and Marilyn lead us from the trail down to the river, where they have discovered a small limestone basin. Two of us can sit and soak, and two can stand under the stream that flows out of the rocks. Bliss! We stand in our underwear in the mud of the Inca Trail with 107-degree water washing over dirty hair and tired bodies. We wave at Cerilio, who watches us from a ledge across the river, where he is (allegedly) gathering firewood.

Wrapped in towels, we tiptoe through the mud, cross the bridge, and return to camp. Tricia and I finally convince Kate that there really is a hot spring. Bill has placed a plastic wading pool right in the middle of the trail with hot water running into it.

Kate looks at the blue-and-white plastic object with a mixture of disapproval, disbelief, and joy. "I can't believe he carried that thing all the way here on a mule!" she says and steps gingerly into the warm water. We leave her there submerged, arms outstretched, eyes closed.

After hanging our clean clothes on a line outside the tent, Tricia sits cross-legged in the grass with a cracked mirror and carefully applies rouge, eyeliner, mascara, and lipstick. I photograph this bizarre activity.

Salami and cheese are on the table, and Pat has concocted a cocktail of pisco, strawberry Jell-o, and fresh lime juice. Raul and I chop onions, apples, and garlic to prepare a chicken curry. Raul tells me that Jaime is his favorite uncle. He asks me if I can understand them when they speak Quechua. I can't. This gives them both great pleasure, for now they can tease and make fun of us without my knowing what they're saying. This is Jaime's first vacation in fourteen years.

When the sun drops behind the surrounding wall of green mountain slopes, the temperature drops with it, and we gather closer to the fire. It's only five o'clock.

After dinner, Bill pulls a bag of marshmallows out of a crate, where they have congealed into a solid mass. The *arrieros*, seated on rocks a polite distance from the fire, watch every move we make in assembling sticky s'mores with graham crackers and chocolate bars. Bill takes them each a sample, and soon their weather-cracked fingers are all stuck together in a wad of melting chocolate and gooey marshmallow. Cerilio eats four.

Pat brings the guitar to the fire, and we sing every Girl Scout/ Campfire Girl song ever written. Judy knows the words to all of them. Verse after verse of "On Top of Old Smokey" drown out the steady roar of the nearby river.

Later, as our circle shrinks, Raul takes the guitar from Pat, lies on his back, and sings softly and slightly off-key to the stars.

The next day is a layover. Judy, Pat, Marilyn, and I hike back up the trail to the small settlement we passed the day before. In twenty minutes, we are out of the canyon. A flat grassy field stretches before us for about a mile, then ends abruptly where yesterday's trail disappears into the steep mountainous jungle. A lonely white peak rises above all else in the blue Andean sky. Salcantay—so far, yet so near—still watches over us.

Crisscrossed by stone fences, the field is partially overgrown with brush and berries. Pigs, chickens, and a dog lie amicably under a tree. A young boy, about ten, who tells us his name is Dante, beckons us to follow him to a store in a mud farmhouse attended by a snaggle-toothed Indian lady who speaks only Quechua. We buy some pisco, ancient "Inca" cigarettes, and a bottle of *trago*. This particular bottle tastes like anise. The change she gives me is so old, torn, and dirty that I can't tell what it is. Both she and her plump, smooth-skinned daughter have large lumps in their cheeks from years of chewing coca leaves. They won't let us take their picture.

On returning to the bottom of the canyon, we find Bill reading a book in his portable "hot tub" in the middle of the trail. When we get to the bridge, we meet a string of burros loaded with sacks of potatoes treading quietly up the trail from the opposite direction. Judy and I scramble out of the way, so as not to scare them.

Judy laughs. "If you think we look scary, how about that big blue thing with a bearded gringo sitting in it right in the middle of their trail?"

"*Allinllachu kakuchanki*," a man and a woman greet us in Quechua. The burros pass us and make their way around the strange object in their path without a sideways glance.

At dusk, we gather again around the fire—clean, rested, and content in this remote but now familiar setting. Raul sits between me and Judy. I envy her youth—smooth skin, thick, brown braid down her back, and (more than anything) a tall, slim body. I am aware of Raul's attraction for Judy, and I envy that, too. He gives us each a kiss and puts his arm around me.

"*Tu eres la mujer mas bonita de todas.* (You are the prettiest woman of all)," he says. In this world of mountains, rocks, dirt, bug bites, cold water, and hot sun, blemishes are hard to hide. Nevertheless, no makeup, diet, hairdo, manicure, or even a facelift could make me feel more beautiful than I do right now.

All I can say is, "*Gracias,*" suspecting that Raul, a natural flirt, is just trying to make me happy, but when he kisses me on the cheek again, I have no doubt of his sincerity.

Chapter Thirteen

ON AND OFF THE TRAIL

▼▼▼▼▼▼▼▼▼▼▼▼▼▼

W e are up before the sun touches our dewy camp. Yesterday's laundry hangs limp and wet on lines strung from trees to tents. Whether they're damp or dry, we stuff underwear, socks, shirts, and scarves into our saddlebags. Our tent is struck, sleeping bags are rolled, and daypacks are filled with water, sunblock, toilet paper, and mosquito repellant. I add my last granola bar and join Brad and Pat, who are watching Bill, Philippe, Jaime, and Raul assist in the daily packing procedure.

Burros, blindfolded by ponchos tied over their eyes, wait to receive their burdens. First, packs with tents, ground cloths, and camp stools are tied on, then boxes of food and cooking utensils are added. When all the loads appear to be evenly distributed, rawhide nets are thrown over the entire load. These are secured by knotted ropes that the *arrieros* wind through and over the cargo. They tie more knots, grunt and mutter in Quechua, yank and pull on the ropes, then tie a final knot.

I remember packing horses with my father. We followed a well-defined method of loading cargo, throwing cinches, and tying

Loading burros for today's ride

Dining table on top

it all together with a diamond hitch. There is no discernible method here, however, as every rope is a different length, and the equipment has been repaired to the point of invention.

"It seems a miracle nothing has fallen off so far," Brad observes.

"Maybe it has," his wife replies.

The *arrieros* pull gently on a few ropes, checking that the cargo is secure. Then, off come the blindfolds, and each burro is free to find his place in the lineup.

Kate and Tricia start off on foot, and we follow soon after on a trail that clings to the side of a steep mountain and winds along its contours through a tunnel of dense foliage. Below us, the Santa Teresa River has joined with the Tortora carrying the melted snow from glaciers high in the Andes away to the Amazon. Its continuous roar inhibits any conversation.

We haven't gone far when Cerilio, who is walking behind Don, the last rider at the end of the line, shouts ahead for us to stop. Don's horse has made a U-turn and is headed back to the green pasture he left behind. Cerilio takes a shortcut straight up the mountainside and intercepts them on the trail. He grabs the reins and sends Don and his recalcitrant beast back in the right direction. They are repositioned near the front, and we move on.

At a wide place in the trail, Antonín motions us to halt again. This time it is to let the pack animals pass. I tighten my reins, remembering the little rodeo that occurred when Brad's horse had the audacity to ride up close to my horse. I wonder why the pack train wasn't sent ahead as usual. The burros trot sedately by, wheezing and grunting under rattling boxes.

"*Mula!*" shouts Mario, with a wave of his red hat, as one veers in my direction. I have a sense of foreboding.

We continue on for a mile in an orderly procession. Lauren chatters behind me, and I force myself to turn around and answer once in a while. Bill points out some potential hazards along the way—protruding rocks to lift a leg over, holes on the downhill side of the trail, and low branches to avoid. We stop again.

Antonín is looking over the edge of the trail through the mass of trees, vines, and bushes to the river far below—at least a hundred feet. A flash of orange tells me that something is down there that shouldn't be. The *arrieros* are talking rapidly with Antonín and Bill, and I learn that one pack animal tried to pass another on the narrow trail, and when their protruding loads collided, one was thrown over the edge.

Questions arise: What if that had been one of us? Is the mule dead? Has he broken a leg? If so, will we have to shoot him? Does anyone have a gun? If not, how does he get out? How will we get his pack up to where we are?

I'm listening to Bill and Antonín discuss the situation when I see an orange box moving through the bushes. With a heroic final crash through the undergrowth, Mario appears with the box strapped to his back. He lowers it quickly to the ground, and without a word, disappears again over the edge. He has made his way up that nearly vertical bank in slippery sandals with fifty pounds on his back.

We wait, seated in our saddles, for about half an hour, passing information on the sequence of events back to our fellow travelers. Slowly, the *arrieros* pull and push the wounded burro up the bank. Breaking branches with machetes at every step, calculating the next maneuver, moving rocks, resting and struggling, back and forth they go until they finally reach the trail. Trembling with exhaustion, probably in shock (just like Kate), the wild-eyed burro returns to his place in line.

Another burro takes the load and we continue, passing a small white cross on the side of the trail where there is no foliage to break a fall. At last, we reach the river's edge and look for a place to cross.

When we reach a spot where the river floods in a wide shallow stream over black rocks, Antonín raises an arm, signaling us to stop and stay where we are. A woman who has been following us with her four burros loaded with potatoes and onions in burlap bags is loudly protesting our long stop on the trail and our slow progress. She wants to pass. Since the trail is narrow, everyone finds a precarious position on the edge of the stream. I check my horse's ears (to detect any sudden mood swings), and at the same time watch a young woman—bright red skirts swirling about her ankles, thick black braids swinging beneath a small derby, multi-colored poncho thrown back over her shoulders—skip across the stream like a skimmed pebble. In one hand, raised high above her head, she holds a whip that whirls and swirls above her burros.

"*Mula!*" she cries, and the burros pick up the pace and clamor up the steep bank. She lifts her skirts, bounds up the bank behind them, and disappears into the jungle.

We follow her across the river, up the bank, and along a trail past waterfalls, through streams, and across green meadows. The river roars relentlessly in the canyon below.

The trail drops again to the bank of the river, and I'm admiring its frothy flow a few feet below me when, once again, we are motioned to dismount—at least, that's how I interpret the vigorous arm waving and yelling, since I can't hear anything. Ahead, the trail is carved out of a rock and passes under a low overhang. I'm glad they warned us. I might have ridden right into it and probably would have been knocked out and off the horse.

Holding my hat, I ride under the rock, and when I look up, I see Raul and Jaime looking across the river at a wet burro on the other side. Jaime explains that the burro was carrying the dining table on top of his load. When the table hit the rock, the animal was flung into the churning rapids. Luckily for him, his load came loose while he struggled in the river, and now it lies miraculously wedged between some rocks near the opposite bank.

Bill notes that our first aid box went down the bank with the first burro, and now our lunch is wedged in those rocks. Raul and the *arrieros* will have to figure out how to get the crate and the burro back on our side.

Why, I wonder, didn't someone walking ahead of the pack animals think of this possibility? I guess, like me, they never looked up.

Ropes are unfurled and flung across the river to the rescuers, who are assisted by some children from a nearby village. *Arriero* ingenuity accompanied by much shouting and tugging finally gets the burro back to our side of the river.

I notice that some of the *arrieros* did not participate in the rescue operation, and I ask Jaime why they didn't help him.

"*Pues, los burros no son de ellos,*" he says. The burros don't belong to those *arrieros*.

Bill adds, "Without their stock, the *arrieros* have nothing. They'll risk their lives to save their own stock, but not someone else's."

We continue down the trail, wondering what will happen next. That's two mishaps. Will there be a third?

In a small green meadow surrounded by willows, we find Kate and Tricia lying in the grass with their hats over their faces. They thought this spot would be a pleasant place to wait for us to catch up.

"Where have you been? We almost went on. We thought we were in the wrong place."

Cinches loosened and horses left to wander, we sit down to a soggy lunch (and later, soggy toilet paper).

Relating the events of the day is always better than living them. After lunch, Kate and the *arrieros* examine the open wounds of the first burro that went down the bank. He is still badly shaken and has a deep gash on his hindquarters. An *arriero* splashes kerosene on the wounds, and Kate adds her gentle touch with some Benadryl.

Chapter Fourteen

TO SANTA TERESA
AND POINTS UNKNOWN

▼▼▼▼▼▼▼▼▼▼▼▼▼▼▼

We arrive at our last campsite with mixed emotions. There is no more rum, no more trago, and a feeling of finality hangs in the air. After a refreshing whirlpool bath in the river, we have an early dinner. The *arrieros* ask for their tips. Mario believes he should be paid extra because my horse stepped on his toe.

Tomorrow, we will depart early to catch the noon train in Santa Teresa. There Antonín, Mario, Cerilio, and the other *arrieros* and their animals will leave us and return on this trail to Mollepata. Raul and Jaime will accompany the rest of us on the train to the Machu Picchu station, and then continue on to Cusco with all of our gear. The rest of us will ride the bus up to the Machu Picchu Hotel: baths, showers, beds, sheets, pisco—and The Ruins!

"Just think, a real bed, dinner in a chair, a bath in hot water," Kate says wistfully—perhaps not really believing any of her dreams will come true. "After the events of this past week . . . who knows?"

"And the ruins," Tricia adds. "Machu Picchu must be one of the greatest archeological mysteries of the world—and we get to see it in clean clothes, with clean hair and no horses."

I haven't thought much about Machu Picchu since we left Cusco, I realize, a bit surprised that I could so easily forget the grand finale of our trans-Andean trek. I'm not sure what I yearn for more—to wander forever in the mountains of Peru, to revel in the luxuries of a hotel, or to lose myself in the mystery of the ancient ruins.

It's warm at this lower elevation, so I take my sleeping bag outside of the tent to sleep under the stars. I gaze up at the Southern Cross, the celestial symbol of the Southern Hemisphere. I think about Osvaldo. Would he have liked this trip? Perhaps he would once he was on it. I know some people would hate it, would never even consider it, but those for whom I feel a deep affinity would love it. I want to share this with someone I love. I vow to bring my children.

The next morning, I awake in a soggy sleeping bag. I had neglected to pull the blue plastic tarp over me, and the morning dew has soaked through. Now there is no time to dry it out, as pack animals and *arrieros* are eager to depart. "No matter," I think. Tonight we'll be in a hotel, and my dirty clothes and wet sleeping bag will be on their way to Cusco.

The well-traveled trail to Santa Teresa descends into a forest of coffee and banana trees. Houses become more frequent. Every yard has a turkey, a flaming red poinsettia tree, and a cement slab for drying coffee beans. It is hot, and all the foliage seems exaggerated. Lantana plants grow in hedges six feet high. Gigantic hibiscus and begonias glow from behind dense foliage. Ferns tower above me, and sunlight sparkles on everything.

Somewhere in the distance, I hear the sound of metal grinding on metal. I wonder if it's a train, but it's unremitting and unchanging, growing louder as we approach.

"What is that dreadful sound?" Judy asks.

"I don't know," I reply. It seems to come from different directions. "Maybe it's a train . . . or a steel mill?"

It rings in my ears all the way to Santa Teresa. "*Raul, que es este ruido?* (What is this noise?)" I ask.

"*Es un bicho, miles de bichos.* (It's a bug, thousands of bugs.)" After further questioning, I discover it's some kind of local cricket.

About an hour away from Santa Teresa, we meet a well-dressed man riding a horse that wears a bright red-and-green *chullo* with tasseled earflaps that hang below the holes cut for his ears. He and Bill exchange polite greetings and questions about our destination. I think I understand him to say that no train has been to Santa Teresa for a week, that all the trains in Peru are on strike, and that no one knows when it will end.

After they bid "*adios*," and he rides on up the trail, I lean forward in my saddle and ask Bill, "What happens if there's no train?"

"I don't know," he replies. "There's no road out of Santa Teresa, I know that." We ride on in silence for a while. "Maybe the strike will end," he says, hopefully.

"And if it doesn't?" I ask

Bill points to a high ridge across the valley. "Somewhere up there is Machu Picchu."

I look across at a vertical wall of impenetrable jungle rising from the river bed to the sky. "No wonder the Spaniards never found it," I reply.

Slowly, the information filters back. There is a strange lack of concern at this point, as we try to accept another deviation from the itinerary as a new possibility, rather than a canceled expectation.

Promptly at eleven thirty, we ride into the dusty town of Santa Teresa. The din of the crickets is strange and irritating. I wonder where they are. They must be very large or very numerous. It bothers me that I can't see one.

We dismount in a sunny square next to the river, which cuts the town in half. I hand the reins to Antonín, wondering if this is the end of the trail or the beginning of a new one. Kate stands

disconsolately alone in the square. Having walked twelve miles
downhill in five hours, she has been fortifying herself with visions
of sitting in a chair in a train, then in a bus, then in a bar, in a bath,
and finally in bed. As Bill describes the situation to her, I can see
Kate looking desperately around for a train, or a bus, or any conveyance to get us out of here, but we have only our wits and the
tired horses. Reality spoils the triumph of arrival.

Raul and Jaime saunter over to us, looking unconcerned. Surely
they'll have a solution. They greet me with open arms, beers, an
orange, and words of encouragement. Jaime seems to know the
area. Raul's youthful optimism is contagious. Something will save
us. It always has so far.

We assemble on the porch of a small store while Bill and
Philippe discuss the situation with the *arrieros*. I have never seen
them all together at once, and it seems there are twice as many as I
remember. At last we are invited to consider the alternatives.

Discussing Exit Options

PLAN A:

We walk uphill for sixteen miles to Machu Picchu and to the Inca Trail. Marilyn says she knows the way. Another group, which arrived in Santa Teresa earlier that day, has already left. Jaime and Raul will wait for the train and return to Cusco with our gear. We will carry day packs and essentials.

Problems:

1. The trail is steep and rocky, and there is no place to camp en route. Therefore, we will have to go the whole way in one day, and Marilyn is doubtful we can make it, unless we leave immediately. Kate and Brad are injured, and all of us are tired.
2. Most of us don't have daypacks, and carrying a saddlebag over my shoulder while hiking up a steep rocky trail is out of the question (I hope).
3. Even if we did find a place to stop and camp, how would we carry food, cooking equipment, and sleeping bags?

Questions:

1. Does Marilyn really know the way? If the strike continues, how will we (and countless other tourists) get back to Cusco from Machu Picchu? How will Raul and Jaime get there? Will they get there before we leave the country? How many people are already stranded in the small hotel at Machu Picchu?

PLAN B:

We can continue with the animals and the *arrieros* down the railroad for twelve or fourteen miles to Chaullay, where there is a road to Cusco. If the strike ends, we can still catch the train near there. If not, perhaps we can find a vehicle traveling on the road to Cusco.

Problems:

1. Thousands of Indians will be descending on Cusco to celebrate Inti Raymi, the Festival of the Sun. With no trains running, those people will be traveling in all available vehicles, so our chances of hitchhiking with all our gear are slim.

2. The festival also attracts tourists, filling vacant rooms in Cusco. Bill suggests an alternative: camping on the outskirts of town in the ruins of Sacsayhuaman with the Indians. This sounds like the worst solution I can imagine—camping with crowds of celebrating Indians, the belligerent drunks of Pisac multiplied by hundreds.

3. Worst of all, we will lose our reservations for two nights at Machu Picchu and might not get there at all.

4. Bill will have to pay the *arrieros* for an extra day.

These alternatives and problems are discussed and considered from every angle. Marilyn, Philippe, and the young and fit (a minority) vote for the Inca Trail. The older and injured opt for the railroad tracks. Both alternatives seem equally impossible to me, but the railroad tracks, at least, are flat.

While we weigh our options, sitting and standing on the steps of the small cantina, the bad *arriero* who led Brad, Don, and Pat off on the first day suddenly takes off for Mollepata with his four horses.

Bill curses him and also himself for having paid him the night before. Now the load of those four pack animals will have to be redistributed among the remaining stock, and there will be four fewer horses to ride if we opt for the railroad trek to Chaullay.

We laze about the local cantina, eat salami and cheese, discuss the situation, drink beer, and wait for something or somebody to tell us what to do. What can any of us contribute to the decision? We have no idea where we are or how far it is to anywhere.

At last, Bill decides to not decide until two o'clock, when the news comes on. Perhaps then he will learn something about the railroad strike that will force a decision.

I'm content to be off the horse, warm in the sun, safe here by the river. I go to explore its rocky shore, dunk my head in the cold water, and climb onto a sunny rock.

Chapter Fifteen

THE WAY TO CHAULLAY

▼▼▼▼▼▼▼▼▼▼▼▼▼▼

At two in the afternoon, riders, horses, and *arrieros* gather in the dusty square in front of the cantina to wait for news of the railroad strike. Even the noisy insects are silent, as if sharing our suspense (or because it's siesta time). Bill steps out of the doorway, looking glum. "No news," he informs us. "They didn't even mention the strike."

Philippe and Marilyn agree that it's too late and too risky to try to intercept the Inca Trail to Machu Picchu, so we pack up the remaining salami and cheese, return bottles to the cantina, and amble down to the riverside, where the *arrieros* squat on their haunches, smoke Inca cigarettes, and accept the news that we are pressing on to Chaullay.

Pat borrows Raul's guitar, goes over to a log, sits down in the shade of a rock wall, and strums a few chords. Surrounded by crates, saddle bags, and an audience of about twenty children perched on rocks and branches above and below her, she sings,

> *"When I was young, I used to sit . . . upon my master's knee*
> *. . . and hand him the bottle when he got dry . . . and brush*
> *away the blue tail fly."*

Dark eyes send glances back and forth, then open wide when we all join in with, *"Jimmy crack corn and I don't care. . . ."*

A little girl in a bright orange dress stands directly in front of Pat. A bottle cap attached to a string tied around her neck swings back and forth as she follows the rhythm, shifting her weight from foot to foot. Her swinging, glossy, black braids shine in the sunlight.

Meanwhile, the *arrieros* are assembling our mountain of gear. Their lack of enthusiasm is evident in the careless way they throw the ropes and tie the loads to the mules, and later it is confirmed by the frequency with which everything comes loose and falls off. At last the loads are redistributed.

Marilyn, Philippe, Kate, and Tricia start out ahead on foot, followed by Judy and Lauren. The rest of us ride single file through town, over a bridge, and past the police station. We stop when Bill, who is bringing up the rear, is asked to present our passports. He tells the officials that we don't have them with us, that this is an unscheduled detour, and that we are tourists on vacation.

As I listen to Bill trying to describe our situation, I wonder if they will believe him. Certainly, no tourists have ever visited this outpost, much less "on vacation." Hopefully, we don't look like terrorists or smugglers.

Bill signals for us to pick up our reins and continue onward. Our destination is an alleged three or four hours' trek down the railroad track to a place called Chaullay, pronounced *chow-lie.* The name, the place, and the surrounding circumstances lead me to imagine a prison camp somewhere in Asia.

I ride off down the railroad tracks, safe in the assurance that no train will come anytime soon. The late-afternoon sun blazes high above the steep mountains that enclose the railroad track on either side, while the Urubamba thunders along below, exploding in white frothy rapids over giant boulders that interrupt its tumultuous course down the canyon.

Soon I have forgotten the name of the town, how far it is, and how long it will take to get there—and, of course, I have no idea what we will find when we do get there. What matters now are the real and spontaneous impressions that surround me—the river, the mountains, the tracks. I don't feel alone. I don't need to know where I'm going. For now, ignorance is optimism.

I catch up with two burros stumbling along the railroad ties. They look back from time to time to see if I'm still there. Passersby greet me as if my presence, although curious, were no more peculiar than anything else that occurs in their lives, and I soon realize these tracks are the main thoroughfare for the people who live in the villages along the way.

The acceptance of odd and extraordinary events as everyday occurrences seems peculiarly Latin to me. In *Aunt Julia and the Scriptwriter*, Mario Vargas Llosa portrays real life as a soap opera and vice-versa, until the reader can no longer tell the difference

Track trek to Chaullay

between reality and fiction. At this moment, I feel somewhat that way myself.

This trip in Peru has taught me that the ability to believe that anything is possible and to accept that not everything has an explanation enhances one's chances of survival. Perhaps I always suspected this truth, but I've never lived it.

The two burros and I overtake a man walking carefully on the rocks beside the tracks. He wears a coat and tie and carries a briefcase in one hand, a folded newspaper in the other.

"*Buenos días,*" he says, removing his tweed hat.

"*Buenos días,*" I reply, looking down from my horse.

"*Donde vas?* (Where are you going?)" He extends an arm in the direction of the animals plodding ahead.

"*No se. No me recuerdo.* (I don't know. I don't remember.)" That must sound pretty dumb, I think, and I try to explain that I can't remember the name of the town. He mentions a few. *Chaullay* sounds familiar, and I nod. He smiles, perhaps reassured that I do have a destination, and I smile back, pleased to learn that Chaullay is actually a place someone would go to.

We bid *adiós* at a cluster of thatched-roof houses tucked into a small arroyo next to a waterfall, and he disappears into the green fronds of banana trees, like a commuter returning home from . . . what?

I catch up with two *arrieros* trying to get the packs straight and the load even on the backs of their three animals. Despite much retying and rearranging, the packs slide over with predictable regularity. When one pack slides under the belly of a skittish mule and sends him leaping, grunting, and farting up a steep rocky slope, Antonín decides he's had enough. He catches the frightened beast and leads him back to flat terrain, where he takes everything off his back to reload.

I ride on ahead, catch up to two burros, and follow them for what seems like an hour, walking slowly and hoping they won't break into a trot. Their loads are loose and lopsided, and the only fear I have in the world at this moment is that their packs will fall off, and I will have to get off my horse and put them back on.

How far ahead are Kate and Tricia? I wonder. *Who is behind me and how far back are they? How far did they say we have to go?* I believe it was twenty kilometers—twelve miles—but that has no meaning in this place. To me, distance is measured by time, but that is meaningless when packs fall off animals, people fall off horses, and horses fall in rivers.

The sound of the river and the buzz of cicadas is deafening, and my joyful optimism is diminishing. The railroad track is getting monotonous, and real questions begin to form: First, where are we going? Then, where will we sleep tonight? And will we have dinner? Will it be in a cantina along the tracks, or in the town that lies somewhere ahead . . . what's it called?

I wonder if I'll ever see Machu Picchu—a place as unattainable now as it was for four centuries.

Pablo Neruda describes that elusive destination in his poem, "The Heights of Machu Picchu."

Then up the ladder of earth I climbed
Through the barbed jungle's thickets
Until I reached you, Machu Picchu.
Tall city of stepped stone,
Home at long last of whatever earth
Had never hidden in her sleeping clothes '
In you two lineages that had run parallel
Met where the cradle both of man and light
Rocked in a wind of thorns.

A tremendous rockslide scars the mountainside from about two thousand feet above me down to the tracks. I look up in awe, as I fall into step with a man in a clean white shirt and polyester pants. I ask him when the slide occurred.

"*Pues, cuando hicieron el camino.* (When they made the road)," he answers, with the lilt of someone more accustomed to speaking Quechua than Spanish.

Road? I ask if the road was going to Machu Picchu.

"*Pués, no se, señora.*"

He doesn't know what the road was for. He tells me there is a hot spring just ahead where one can bathe and wash clothes. He is a traveling salesman returning home from a day's work. His house is just below the spring under some banana and coffee trees. A group of children with glistening wet hair and shiny faces greet him, and he disappears down yet another path toward the river.

I am alone again with my two animals. It's almost dusk, and the mules know it is feeding time. They wander off the trail that runs beside the track, searching for grass. I mustn't let them fall behind. We must keep moving.

One crosses the track, and the other turns around and starts wandering in the wrong direction.

"*Heeyah! Heeyup, hup, hup!*" I remember the sounds from driving cattle on the ranch in California. The mules return to the trail and break into a trot, their packs bouncing and rattling loosely on their bony backs.

As I encourage them along with whistles and grunts, I think about my father. His memory has often been with me on this trip. So many long dusty rides we shared in those golden hills, so many cows to chase after—canyons to gallop down, bending under low branches, up steep hills with the saddle slipping back and the horse running out of control. Moments of peril seemed like high adventure with him. I remember following his boot prints for hours through mountains and streams of the California Sierra, hoping I was still on the right trail. He was never concerned that I was far behind, maybe lost. I asked him once why he never waited.

"That way I know you'll keep coming," he replied.

If he didn't consider me lost, I guess I wasn't. My father had a benevolent unconsciousness when it came to raising children. He treated us all as equals—boys, girls, older or younger. He never told us how to ride a horse. We just did it. We were not afraid because he wasn't, and we assumed we could do anything because he always let us try. He seldom told us something was dangerous, and he believed only careless people got hurt.

He gave us the confidence to try everything. Our failures had their own inherent consequences, and we learned from those.

How far I am right now, I think, from those familiar California hills.

Antonín catches up with me and urges the animals along by throwing small stones. Glad to be relieved of this responsibility, I go on ahead and join Don and Bill. We decide to trot for a while, but find it to be like sitting on a four-legged vibrating machine and soon give up.

We're still laughing when a short, stocky woman clambers up the bank from the river and staggers along the track a ways. Dressed like a doll in a bright blue full skirt, white shirt, black vest, and white bowler hat, she flashes us a cockeyed grin, lurches forward, and nearly topples on her face under my horse. I pull him quickly to one side and wait to see what will happen next. Returning to a perpendicular position, she extends an arm in a grand gesture, bows, and steps aside so we can pass.

"*Viva el trago*," Don says.

By six o'clock, the sun has retreated to some far-off horizon. Twilight lingers in the canyon for only half an hour. I remember that Inti Raymi, winter solstice and the shortest day of the year in the Southern Hemisphere, is only a few days away.

Bill, Don, and I arrive at a river that flows down the mountain to join the Urubamba. The bridge used by trains is not sturdy enough for animals, so Antonín, always there when we need him, leads us through the bushes on a path down to the river's edge. The current looks strong, and I wonder how deep it is.

Antonín hops from rock to rock along the edge, moving upstream until he finds a place to cross. My horse's mother is wandering riderless downstream below the bridge. I can tell he is anxious to join her, but downstream is not where I want to go. I know we must cross upstream, where Antonín crossed, but I also know it is impossible to control my horse when he wants to be with Mother.

I take my feet out of the stirrups and lift them above the water, moving gingerly downstream toward Mother, who cooperates by moving upstream toward us. With little nudges and circling reins, I head her back in the direction of the steep muddy trail that I hope leads up to the road. Suddenly, she veers to the right, lurches, struggles up the bank, and disappears into the bushes.

My horse leaps out of the water right behind her, struggles, slips, and falls on his stomach. I could easily step off, but my instinct is to stay in the saddle while the poor horse thrashes about and slides back into the river. Then I do get off. Stumbling around on unseen rocks in muddy water up to mid-thigh, I curse the wretched beast as he takes off up the trail without me. I crawl up on all fours behind him. Antonín looks dismayed, but I assure him the horse is fine.

Chapter Sixteen

GRINGOS PERDIDOS

▼▼▼▼▼▼▼▼▼▼▼▼▼▼

Hands trembling, I hand the reins to Judy. "You can have him, Judy. I think I'll walk for a while."

The riders go on ahead, and I return to the trail that runs beside the tracks on the riverside. Pack animals wander back and forth across the tracks, trying to nibble on the other side, dropping their packs and stopping whenever an *arriero* isn't clucking or pelting them with stones.

In order to avoid this annoying and uneven pace, a group of us walk on the raised ties in the middle of the track. Our heads are bowed in concentration, my wet shoes sloshing to the rhythm of the railroad ties, which seem to flow backward beneath my feet. Shadowy bushes drift by in my peripheral vision. The outline of mountains high on the horizon fades into the darkening sky, and the river is only a sound. All that has become familiar in this day is gone. An almost full moon shines its pearly beams along silver tracks, and I'm sure we have been traveling for three, maybe four hours by now.

As if reading my thoughts, Pat asks Bill how far we have gone. They speculate about that, and how much farther it might be, and how far ahead are the others.

Others? I'd forgotten about the others.

"What's the name of that town again, Pat?"

"Chaullay."

If I thought it were significant, wouldn't I remember the name? If I cared, wouldn't I be making careful estimations of time and distance and be concerned about where we will eat and sleep, and how we will get back to Cusco, and what will happen to us when we get there?

How have I fallen into this semiconscious state of not knowing or caring where we are going? Why do I feel so completely alive in the present—so free from the responsibility of having to know where I am and what I will do next? *Something like the minutes before you drown or freeze to death*, I imagine Kate saying.

I fall into step with Raul and two burros.

"*Como vas, mujer linda?* (How're you doing, pretty woman?)"

"*Bien, bien.*" Being called a pretty woman at this moment in this place reaffirms my conviction that I belong here on these railroad tracks and inspires me with enough energy to walk straight over the Andes.

He asks me questions about my family, and I tell him about my children and my father and the ranch and some horses I have known. He listens with interest, and I learn that his grandmother died last year of peritonitis after an appendectomy. She had been the most important person in his life until then, and it seemed so unjust that she should die of an appendectomy—or that she should die at the age of fifty-five. She was a healthy woman.

"*Ahora mi padre is la cabeza de la familia, y algún día será yo.* (Now my father is head of the family, and someday it will be me.)"

Raul has a strong sense of family responsibility, as protector of his younger sister and her children and of his little brother. He asks me about my husband, and I tell him he, too, plays the guitar.

He asks if I would like him to be here.

"*Pienso que no.* (I don't think so)," I reply. He seems to understand that and asks no more questions.

He tells me that he would never let his wife go anywhere without him. That would mean he didn't love her. I try to explain that it's different in North America, but I can tell he's not convinced.

Although Raul is studying to be a civil engineer, he doesn't think he will ever find a job in his country.

"*No hay dinero para hacer nada. Gano mas trabajando con mi padre en turismo.* (There is no money to build anything. I earn more working with my father in tourism.)"

We continue chatting about our families, responsibilities, friends, relationships, and things we like—much like neighbors who have known each other for a long time. Pat, Brad, and Bill join us, and after a while, I fall behind with my musings and two mules.

Suddenly they stop. Ears pricked and heads alert, they stare into the darkness. Something out there has frightened them, but I can't see, hear, or even imagine what it could be. I shout, wave my arms, throw a few stones at them, and they bolt past the invisible object. I walk in the middle of the tracks, as if the rails on either side will protect me from whatever lurks between me and the unseen river. A child-like sense of *something's out there* materializes, as a shadowy mechanical monster slowly takes form as a bulldozer. A little farther down the track, a young man sits on his motorcycle, watching our parade of meandering pack animals, tired riders, and walkers.

"Dear God," I pray, "don't let him start the motor and send the mules galloping back to Santa Teresa."

"*Hola! Que es este grupo?* (Hello, what is this group?)" he asks.

"*Un grupo de gringos perdidos.* (A group of lost gringos)," I answer.

Obviously, we are not a group of trekkers on a planned excursion down the railroad tracks of "Inner Peru." Perhaps he thinks we're refugees or prisoners on a forced march.

"*Donde van?* (Where are you going?)" he asks.

I was hoping he wouldn't ask that. "*Al proximo pueblo.* (To the next town)," is my clever reply.

"*Ah, Santa Maria.*"

Santa Maria? I'm not sure if that was an expletive or a place. It doesn't sound familiar, not sinister enough. He tells me he knows a good hotel and suggests we meet there. What a wonderful idea! Immediately I envision myself in a dimly lit café, leaning back in a wooden chair with a cold beer and a plate of anything. . . . A handsome stranger in jeans dirtier than mine is fascinated with my stories of adventure and suffering.

A glowing light in the distance interrupts my fantasy, and I walk hopefully to a grassy clearing by the side of the tracks. I squint at what appear to be the outlines of thatched roofs at the edge of the green. Familiar faces and voices bring me back to the present. Brad, Pat, Bill, Judy, and Lauren lie about in various positions of repose on top of packs and bundles. Animals graze around them. They tell us they have not seen Kate, Tricia, Marilyn, or Philippe.

"They must be ahead," I say, "as they surely aren't behind."

Jaime, whom I haven't seen since we left Santa Teresa, comes forward to embrace me, offering a supportive swig of rum and a smile that warms the night.

Noisy, high-spirited children surround us. They seem almost hysterical, so ardent and sincere is their welcome. They hold our hands and bring us nuts and bananas and invite us to spend the night in their village. They tell us they haven't seen our friends pass through, so they must be behind us. We know that is impossible— at least I think it is. They assure us there is no place to sleep in

Chaullay, no place for animals to graze, no food, no water. It is a terrible place with lots of trucks and bandits.

This energetic encounter makes me tired, so I lie down on the soft grass and lean against a pack. How nice it would be to stay and sleep here on the grass. Damn the others for walking so far ahead of us. We have to get up and continue in the dark to that place with the elusive name.

On my feet again, I wave reluctantly to the good people who live here and return to the dark tracks, darker now that the moon is obliterated intermittently by eucalyptus trees.

The railroad ties seem uneven, and I can't walk on them now without missing.

"*No está muy lejos ahora, niña.* (It's not very far now, child.)" Jaime's voice is deep and soothing by my side. I wonder why he calls me "niña." He is only two years older than I am. He shines his flashlight ahead on the tracks.

"*Cuidado.* (Be careful)," he says each time I stumble. About an hour ago, I wasn't tired or very concerned about where we were going or when we'd get there. Trekking along the tracks in the jungle of Peru was fine with me, but after resting in that field, the adrenalin that held off fatigue has vanished, and now I'm weary like I never imagined. Unsure of my ability to put a foot squarely on each railroad tie, I use the beam of the flashlight as my guiding light, as the world around us dissolves in darkness.

An hour later, we approach a town, and Jaime turns off his flashlight.

People . . . lights . . . activity . . .

From our perspective in the dark railroad bed three feet below street level, the town of Santa Maria above and on either side of us looks like a movie set from *Oklahoma!* I feel like the unseen audience, and it wouldn't surprise me if all of the people up there suddenly started *singin' 'n' dancin' 'n' leanin' on their brooms.*

I want to be up there in one of those adobe buildings where people are eating, cooking, and gossiping in their lighted shops, bars, and homes. Jaime boosts himself up to street level and walks above me, asking questions of passersby about campsites, distances, the train strike, and if they have seen others like us pass through. He returns to the trench, and we wave good-bye, as we walk offstage into the darkness. I wonder where my man on the motorcycle is, if he's waiting for me in the hotel.

When I ask Jaime what he has learned, the only information I get is "not far"—a response you can always count on.

About half a mile beyond Santa Maria, the tracks veer to the left, and we leave them to follow a dirt road to the right, which leads to a metal suspension bridge. Antonín waits there to warn us that we must lead our horses across one at a time.

I watch apprehensively as Don dismounts to lead his horse across. He takes a few tentative steps, and the bridge heaves, groans, and sways. The noise of hooves on metal reverberates above the roar of the rapids below. Don hesitates, and two unattended pack mules start across behind him.

"*Ay, caramba!*" Jaime mutters, as he leaps forward to try to stop them.

Antonín waves his arms to drive them off, but this only drives them onward towards Don, who is now midway on the bridge.

He'll be trampled, I fear. He can't possibly outrun them on the swaying and undulating bridge. The mules try to pass, and one tries frantically to squeeze past Don's horse, shoving the horse against Don, who is pressed into the woven wire sides. I see him look down at the water, as the moonlight chases the swirling foam away into darkness.

With little effort on their part, the mules reach the other side and begin to graze contentedly. Don leads his horse the rest of the way and waits for us to cross. I make sure no unattended pack animals are behind me.

"That was some bridge," Don remarks.

"Weren't you scared?" I ask.

"Yes, I guess so, but it happened so fast." He looks back at the bridge and says, "I think, after this trip, nothing will ever scare me again."

A little way farther, a lonely boarded-up train station stands deserted by the side of the tracks.

"*Llegamos*. (We're here)," Jaime announces.

"*Llegamos?*" Is this it?

We continue uphill to a grim and dusty flat area in front of a closed warehouse. A rambling wood structure by the road has a light on inside. There are no trees and hence no bathroom. It is just the way I always imagined a place called Chaullay would look.

Chapter Seventeen

NOW WHAT?

▼▼▼▼▼▼▼▼▼▼▼▼▼▼▼▼

Horses with empty saddles and mules and burros with their lopsided loads almost dragging in the dirt mill about in the dark. Exhausted riders search for their animals to remove their personal belongings from the saddlebags before the *arrieros* pull everything off and carry it away.

My little gray beast stands next to her mother, looking more tired than I am. When I go to give her a good-bye pat, I remember to retrieve the saddlebag with my personal possessions. Finding both sides open, I'm pleased to discover Kate's bottle of rum and my camera lying safely in the bottom with an empty water bottle and a long-forgotten hairbrush. I untie the bag on both sides and sling the whole thing over one shoulder, wondering how long it has been open and why everything hasn't fallen out.

Antonín appears by my side like a faithful ghost.

"*Buena suerte, Señora Eddy*. (Good luck)," he says while removing his saddle from his horse. We embrace and bid *adiós*, and he drags his tack off to the warehouse where a truck waits with its ramp down. Is this something they arranged in advance? The *arrieros* load their animals, close the ramp, and wave good-bye to those of us who are paying attention. Bill tells me they will go back to Santa Maria for the night, probably get drunk in that wonderful town where the man with the motorcycle is waiting for me.

Judy and I carry our saddlebags to the designated "safe place" in front of the warehouse. We learn that there is a cantina where we can eat, and that Kate and Tricia are waiting there. The thought of food and reuniting with friends revives our sagging spirits, and we shuffle off through the dust to embrace Kate and Tricia in the dim light of a dilapidated tin building. Since we left camp at seven that morning, Kate has walked the entire thirty miles. The rest of us have traveled by foot and by horse for fourteen hours.

"Come on, let's go find a bush," Judy says, pulling a roll of toilet paper out of her pocket and waving it in the air.

We leave Kate and Tricia with the rum bottle and walk to the warehouse, making our way around the back. I hear noises inside and briefly wonder who or what is in there. It's very dark, as clouds have covered the moon.

"Here's a little doorway," Judy says, unzipping her jeans and squatting. Just then, loud and savage barking sends us leaping backwards. The door rattles and bangs as claws scratch desperately on the other side of the door. I envision the door flying off its hinges and a German shepherd leaping at my throat.

"Jesus, that was scary," Judy says. "Now where do we go?"

"Here, by the edge of the road," I suggest. "It's so dark, who cares where we go?"

"I can't see more than a foot in front of me," she says.

"I'm here, just off the road." We peer into the darkness. "Do you hear a river?" I ask.

We try to get closer into the brush, but it's too thick to penetrate, so we return to the clearing by the road. I sense some great space in front of me. The moon comes out from behind a cloud.

"Oh, my God!"

We are about ten inches from the edge of a precipice and a thousand feet above the Urubamba, where the moonlight illuminates its swift and steady flow through the jungle.

"Bet you never thought a simple thing like peeing in the bushes could be fatal," Judy says with a wry laugh.

"I think I'm too tired to even pee," I answer, and we begin to laugh uncontrollably, hysterically.

We return to the wood-and-tin structure that serves as a general store/bus station/post office/information center in front, and a café in the rear. A small eating area has been set up for us in the back. Bill and Philippe are negotiating with the proprietress for dinner. Philippe kicks at the guinea pigs he has disturbed from their warm spot under the stove. We lift our weary limbs over wooden benches and boxes and sit down at a table covered with a yellow plastic cloth. For the first time, Pat's face looks drawn and resigned. Brad winces and holds his side as he swings a leg slowly over the bench.

A feast of rice, potatoes, tomatoes, and onions with a fried egg on top is served on tin plates, accompanied by warm beer, rum, and Inca Cola. A mixture of relief and exhaustion drives us into a state of hilarity. Judy and I can barely coordinate laughter and eating at the same time.

"To the end of the 'long march'!" Kate proposes a toast, and we lift our tin cups.

Kate tells me there were times when she thought she wouldn't make it.

"I don't know what was worse," she says, "the pain at every step, the complete weariness of nights without sleeping, walking so far for so long, or the stress of not knowing where we were or when it would end."

"Oh, Kate, I'm so sorry about your back. I can't imagine what it would be like to walk all this way in pain," I say. "It was bad enough if you were completely healthy and super fit."

"I think we should have stopped somewhere and spent the night. This was too far to go in one day," she says.

"Yes, but no one knew how far it would be," Tricia joins in. "For me, the worst part was being alone on those tracks with the Sendero Luminoso all around."

"Oh, dear," I say. "I forgot all about the Senderos."

Oddly, I never felt alone. Am I a fool, that I never suspected I was in any danger? I can't imagine the pain Kate has endured, can't summon up enough sympathy to alleviate her pain, can't comprehend Tricia's fears. I feel emotionally alienated.

OUR HOTEL TONIGHT IS A CEMENT slab by the warehouse. The coffee beans that dry there by day in the sun have been swept aside to make room for our tents.

"At least it's level," remarks Kate.

My sleeping bag is wet and clammy—just as it was when I stuffed it in the sack this warm, sunny morning, when I thought I was going to Machu Picchu. It's too hot to sleep inside the tent,

Kate contemplating her bed for tonight

so I drag my bag and Ensolite pad to a place between our tent and Pat and Brad's. Lights from the warehouse shine down on our gray cement campsite. Dogs bark inside the warehouse, and trucks come and go through the night. Brad is snoring in the tent next to me, because his cracked ribs necessitate him sleeping on his back.

I can hear Judy and Raul giggling as they drag their sleeping bags out of the overhead lights. I envy her youth and ability to fall easily into the casual intimacy of Raul's affection.

Mosquito bites itch, and the lining of the bag feels damp on my hot, sweaty flesh. How can I be so tired and not fall asleep?

At seven o'clock, Bill awakens us with the news that he's found a truck going to Cusco. Jaime and Raul have gone with the driver to the neighboring village to get gas and insure the truck's swift return.

We pull ourselves together and reassemble for breakfast, which is the same as dinner. Stray chickens and guinea pigs wander under the table, hoping we'll drop a crumb.

Philippe joins us. "This place is full of thieves," he says. "Don't leave any of your gear out of your sight." I learn that he and Bill, Raul, and Jaime took turns through the night guarding our pile of gear.

After breakfast, tents are struck, packed, and stacked in front of the warehouse. Pat, Kate, Tricia, and I join Judy and the other women in the search for a "bathroom." We walk all around the warehouse, looking for a sheltered nook, tree, or bush over two feet high—any uninhabited corner. Since we are the objects of much curiosity in this community of about a hundred adults and countless children, it is impossible to disappear in broad daylight. Modesty is a nuisance.

A church and a school stand close to the warehouse, and more houses are scattered across the hill behind, becoming denser around a little square with a well. As the day grows longer and warmer, our interest in the village diminishes, and we settle ourselves on and around the packs in the shade of the warehouse. Trucks come and go, loading sacks of coffee beans. Women sell us salted lima beans and smile sympathetically from a polite distance.

We idle away an hour playing with the children, trading words, writing names, drawing pictures. They are dressed in gray uniforms, and their school is just a few hundred yards away. However, school seems to be taking place in front of the warehouse today.

An older man, presumably a teacher, talks to us in Quechua. He seems to be saying something important, so I ask him if he speaks Spanish.

He does, and he tells me that the Choquechaca bridge is a few miles away, and he would like to take us there. I propose this to Bill and the group, but no one dares risk missing the truck to Cusco, so we politely decline.

John Hemming mentions this bridge frequently in his history *Conquest of the Incas*, as does every Inca historian. It was the main escape route for Manco Inca fleeing Ollantaytambo in 1537 and for all fleeing Incas thereafter until the end of their existence. It was the last gateway to the remote and wild interior where first Manco, then Sayri Tupac, then his half-brother Titu Cusi, and last his half-brother Tupac Amaru held out until the Spaniards finally routed them from their jungle stronghold at Vilcabamba. This bridge over the Urubamba was heavily guarded, and many Spaniards and Incas lost their lives in its defense. During Manco's reign, Pizarro led an unsuccessful raid on Vilcabamba. Manco Inca continued to harass the Spaniards in countless raids until his death in 1544.

From Vilcabamba, Titu Cusi carried on skillful negotiations with the Spaniards for ten years. He convinced the Spaniards that he would soon give up Vileabamba and join his conquerors peacefully. He had no intention of doing this, and he died in Vilcabamba in 1571. The last chapter of Peter Frost's guidebook, *Exploring Cusco*, describes "Vilcabamba—Refuge of the Rebel Incas." Unfortunately,

I read Frost's book later when I was thousands of miles away from Chaullay, and was sorely disappointed that I didn't know all of this before I spent the morning sitting on that platform eating lima beans and drawing pictures with the possible descendants of Tupac Amaru. It is unlikely I'll ever get back to Chaullay to see the bridge at Choquechaca.

BILL IS STANDING ON A PLATFORM eating a papaya. Hundreds of dark eyes stare up at him in reverent silence. Nine o'clock comes and goes with no sign of a truck. Lolling about on our mountain of gear, we discuss the possibilities of tonight's accommodations. No one mentions that it could be here in Chaullay. A few families have been waiting all day for a bus or a truck to take them to Cusco. I have begun to take it for granted that getting out of these predicaments is as easy as getting into them. Kate and Pat are not so sure.

"I'm exhausted by always changing our plans," Pat says.

"If you don't have a plan in the first place, you won't have to change it," I suggest.

"I can't live that way," she replies.

I agree that plans are good, but that they often go awry, especially while traveling, and we have to accept that. Before we can pursue this tired subject any further, the sound of a truck brings us all to our feet. Raul and Jaime, victorious grins on their sun-darkened faces, ride in the front seat.

"Do you think it will take us to Cusco?" Pat asks no one in particular.

"I wonder what kind of road it is," Brad mutters. "How far is it?"

"Who's driving it?" Don asks.

Has anyone ever been this way before? I wonder.

The arrival of a truck creates a new list of alternatives. We discuss these while loading the crates for what we hope will be the last time. Duffels, packs, and saddlebags are tossed on top, and we clamber aboard. Cerilio appears and greets us soberly as he climbs the slats on the side of the truck. Kate and Brad have checked the bald tires and located a spare. It appears to be flat. No one, not even Jaime, has been over this road before. Until last night in Santa Maria, he didn't even know there was a road. The driver estimates a ten-to-fourteen-hour trip. As the back gate is pounded into place, the truck begins to roll backwards.

Now what?

The question is answered by a jerk and a jolt as the engine starts, and we are on our way.

Chapter Eighteen

TODO PERU!

▼▼▼▼▼▼▼▼▼▼▼▼▼▼▼▼

We have all staked out our territory — comfort, view, and proximity to one's pack being priorities. Marilyn and Philippe go for the view from a box on top of the cab. Don and Jaime opt for a real seat inside the cab with the driver, where they might have some control over our destiny—or at least information on our progress. Bill, Brad, Judy, Lauren, and Kate choose the top of the heap, their backs supported by the slats of the truck. They have a view to the sides and the rear. The rest of us make our nests wherever we can fit between saddles and crates and newly acquired boxes of produce. Bill invites Tim, a young British lawyer who has also walked from Santa Teresa to Chaullay, to join us.

When everyone and everything is on board, the truck roles backward, the engine engages, gears grind, and we climb up and away from the hot, green jungle, leaving a cloud of dust between us and Chaullay.

At last, we are on our way, I think, as we round a sharp curve, and everyone shifts to the right, then left. Then we stop.

The driver takes the back gate down. Puzzled, but content to have made some progress, we climb out.

"*Vamos a tomar una cerveza.* (Let's have a beer)," Raul says.

"Why are we stopping here?" Brad and Pat ask in unison.

"*No sé. Para comprar bananas, quizás.* (I don't know. To buy bananas, perhaps.)"

"Jaime says the driver wants to buy bananas," Pat affirms as she makes herself comfortable on the outcrop of a stone wall.

"I think Bill is buying them for the trip," Brad offers.

I can see Jaime and the driver moving crates out of a shed.

"What are all the bananas for?" Kate asks Bill.

"We're taking them to Cusco."

We also load some extra barrels of gas. Bill requests they be lashed to the slats at the far end of the truck bed, and he asks everyone not to smoke.

We climb back in the truck, and a bee stings me.

Two crates of bananas and two more male passengers join us. Pat eyes them suspiciously.

"Do you think they'll be looking for a hotel in Cusco?" she asks, worried they might get the last two beds.

"They probably have family in Cusco," Raul replies as he sinks down into a crouch next to the two men. "They're going to Cusco for Inti Raymi."

Dressed in clean white shirts, pressed pants, and polished black shoes, they appear to be young, maybe twenty. One of them slicks down his shiny, wet hair with a little comb, and they crouch side by side next to the gas barrels.

Once again the truck rolls backward, jolts to life, and moves slowly forward. We return to our former positions. It is warm and sunny on top of the truck, and we're on our way to Cusco. High spirits prevail over minor discomforts and vague misgivings. Pat, standing next to Raul and the two men at the back, is the only one not sitting on top of the packs with an aerial view. Brad entreats her to join him in our happy heap.

"No thanks, I'm just fine right here," she says.

Climbing ever upward, the dirt road is only a little wider than the truck. As on many mountain roads in Peru, there is a day designated for each direction of travel. I guess today is up, as we meet no one coming down. Frequently, smaller, faster trucks are blocked behind us. They honk impatiently until we reach a space wide enough for half a vehicle to pass. So far, no one has gone over the edge, and I'm glad our driver lets *them* take the outside path. A lush green canyon falls away about a thousand feet below. The higher we go, the tighter the turns, and the steeper the sides of the canyon become until it is perpendicular.

We have been traveling about an hour when we are stopped at a wide place in the road. I notice a few thatched roof buildings by a muddy spring and more tin buildings with tin roofs on the other side. Short men in uniforms, carrying guns, come out to the truck and squint up at us from the road below. They tell us we will have to get down and let them inspect the truck.

They ask for our passports. I find it hard to take them seriously, and since we don't have our passports, they tell us the number and country of citizenship will do. I make up a number, and they write it down.

Later, when I tell Kate this, she informs me that this is how the US government searches for missing tourists when they have been kidnapped. If we are victims of a terrorist attack, and the government has the wrong number, no one will know what happened to us.

While they search the truck, we go to inspect the food being served at the edge of the road. Short, plump women in blue dresses with dirty aprons try to tempt us with warm potatoes, *chicha*, and *anticucho* sizzling on a stick. Jaime and Raul share a beer.

"*Que buscan los soldados?* (What are the soldiers looking for?)" I ask.

"*Contrabanda*," is his all-inclusive answer.

We return to the truck and find that most of our packs and bulging duffels have been moved, and after two more of these inspection stops, nothing is where it was when we started. The soft pack behind my head is gone, and in its place is the corner of a metal box. Judy's feet fill the slot where my shoulder fit before. At each jerky stop, Judy slides downward until she is almost on top of me.

Tricia, Judy, and I are embedded high in the center of the load, where we have a panoramic view of mountains on either side and the road disappearing below and behind us. We have no idea where our packs or saddlebags are, but it's warm and sunny, and we're on our way to Cusco—so who cares?

We stop for lunch in the middle of the road, since there is no place to pull off. If anyone wants to pass here, they will just have to join us for lunch. A small wooden structure protrudes from the edge of the cliff. Inside, a curious proprietor supplies us with beer and coke. Tim, the hitchhiking Brit, stands in the doorway, daintily holding a pink china tea cup of coca tea. We spread our picnic of anchovies, sardines, salami, and the last of the Pisac bread (now over a week old) on some oil barrels by the side of the building.

It is pleasant here, gazing down into the jungle. I try to imagine Manco Inca fleeing down the river with the Spaniards hacking through the vegetation in slow pursuit. Kate comes over and stands next to me.

"Do you know what I'm going to tell people when I get home?" she asks.

"No, what?"

She rolls up her sleeve with a delicate gesture and says, "When they ask what I thought of Machu Picchu, I'm going to say, 'Machu Picchu? That tourist place? Everyone goes there. We went to much less touristy places. We went to authentic villages along the railroad tracks. We stayed in remote jungle settlements, where no tourists have ever been.'"

Tricia and I are glad to see Kate has regained her sense of humor, and we relish the image of envious looks on our friends' faces when we return to tell our tales.

"How will we ever describe this?" Tricia asks.

"It's not over yet," Kate reminds us.

Back in the truck, we continue winding back and forth in a series of endless switchbacks. The jungle is far below, and vegetation becomes more sparse the higher we climb. The top of the pass is not yet in sight. Brad calculates that we started out at about five thousand feet, and we must have climbed to about ten thousand.

Bill says, "It looks more like twelve thousand, because we are beginning to see clumps of *ichu* grass. That grass only grows in the *puna* region, which is between snowline and about twelve thousand feet."

I remember walking through the yellow clumps of *ichu* in the open plain above our camp at the foot of Soray. There, it grew in thick tussocks about two feet high. Here, there are little tufts of about two inches. The *arrieros* say it is good grazing food for llamas and alpacas.

Far below, I can barely make out the bends of the river, while across the landscape surrounding our lonely ascent, a melancholy and barren land extends as far as I can see.

When our driver swerves to avoid fallen rocks, potholes, and other unseen obstacles, Judy's foot presses on my neck, and I move away, pushing a tin box into Tricia's knee. I look up at Kate in her corner and wonder if she will be paralyzed in her stiff upright position. Cerilio, who now sits below her, looks pained but no less stoic than Kate. Perhaps the mixture of rum, codeine, and high altitude has the same effect on Kate as chewing coca leaves has on Cerilio.

"*El Paso de Málaga*," someone announces.

Bill estimates it to be about sixteen thousand feet.

"Planes don't fly a lot higher than this," he says.

We disappear from earth into a cloud, and I savor the sensation of being on top of the world. I can't see up or down. I can imagine what is below and behind us, but I can't imagine what lies ahead.

Rain begins to fall, softly at first, then steadily. Icy water dribbles down the back of my neck. Still wearing sleeveless T-shirts, we all begin to search for our packs, saddlebags, more clothes. With a great deal of effort and disruption of those around me, I manage to get my long-sleeved shirt out from underneath Raul.

All of us are wet by now, and Pat, wearing flip-flops, can't find her shoes or socks.

"They were right there by the oil drum." She points to an empty floor space. Brad offers her his socks, but she declines, insisting he find her shoes.

I find my sleeping bag, which I had not packed when we left Chaullay because I thought it was too wet. I throw it across the middle of the truck, covering me and Tricia and Judy's bare legs. The rain increases, and I glance up at Kate, who is wrapped in a plastic poncho. *Smart woman*, I think.

Cerilio looks grimmer than ever—positively miserable. When he leans forward, water runs off his hat brim onto his bare sandaled feet. Still wearing the alpaca sweater Kate gave him, he opens a little pouch that is tied around his waist and scoops out a new supply of coca leaves. The two hitchhikers have lightweight jackets on. They pull their thin collars up. Pat stands shivering in her shorts beside them and Raul.

"Pat, come and sit here with us. It will be warmer," Tricia pleads. Pat shakes her head.

"Do you want to come up here with me?" her husband suggests.

"No. I'll be okay down here."

"Raul, why don't you come and sit here. There's plenty of room," Tricia invites him. "Besides, you can keep us warm."

"*La señora Pat . . .*" he gestures in our direction, but she shakes her head.

Raul crawls in between me and Tricia. It's more crowded, but warmer.

Judy relocates her foot under Raul's neck. She is nestled comfortably with Tim in the row above us. My left arm is now asleep, and I am trying to find it when I see a little furry thing burrowing next to Tricia's nose.

"What's that?" I exclaim in horror. It's Raul's hand in an alpaca mitten. Relieved, I lean back with my head on his arm.

We are still climbing—very slowly. The switchbacks are steeper and shorter. The rain turns to snow, and the truck comes to a groaning halt.

Now what?

I pray that the engine won't die and that we won't have to roll backward over a cliff to start it. It occurs to me that we might have some mechanical malfunction and have to walk from here.

The driver gets out with a windshield wiper in his hand and cleans the front window, then returns to the cab. The engine dies. Just as I'm thinking we should all get out, the truck rolls backward to within a few feet of the edge of the cliff, sputters to life, and we move forward.

With one arm out the window wiping and the other wrestling with the steering wheel, our intrepid driver continues coaxing his truck upward. Bill uncovers a large blue tarpaulin and throws it across the entire truck bed like a roof. It's a great relief from the snow and sleet, but torture for those who suffered first from acrophobia and now from claustrophobia.

I lie shivering between Raul and Tricia, no longer concerned with Pat's cold feet, Kate's sore back, or all the cold, wet people who remain outside the tarp. Helplessly confined in my cocoon in the clouds, I accept that there is nothing I can do but wait and see—so I wait, without seeing, for what will happen next.

Suddenly, Bill rips away the tarpaulin. He stands astride a mound of wet packs, his beard covered with snow. "This is the top—sixteen thousand feet," he announces. "You've got to see this sight." I wriggle up and out of my hole.

Outside the truck, barren misty mountaintops fall away into the clouds. It seems a place so desperately desolate that perhaps no human has ever been here, but this is Peru, and a small family of ragged children and parents not much taller than their children wave from a black smoky hut. They wear colorful chullos and brown alpaca ponchos.

The fog lifts, and alpenglow spreads its rosy tint over snow fields and mountaintops to the north, then washes the lower slopes with shades of gold and orange. Mt. Veronica, nineteen thousand feet high, rises above the scene like an icy jewel in an indigo sky. Her glaciers, visible at eye level, hang frozen in time.

"This is *todo Peru*," Bill says as his gaze sweeps across mountains, glaciers, sky, and then down into the valley below.

The sky is not above us. We are in it. Stars twinkle at eye level and seem so close you could pluck them like sparkling plums in space.

Down. It's a new direction. Kate, from her position at the front of the truck, turns stiffly, just enough to look over the edge.

"You won't believe this." She tries to sound nonchalant. "It's straight down to nothing. There's no *there* down there."

After the truck makes the first very slow turn, the view is on my side. The icy peak of Veronica, its glaciers bathed in moonlight, rises slightly above eye level on the horizon. The moon hangs like a small white ornament next to it, its ghostly light glimmering on miles of muddy switchbacks that wind like wet velvet snakes into the abyss below. I cannot see an end. I wonder briefly if Don was kidding when he told me at lunch that the brakes didn't work. It never seemed terribly important, as long as we were going uphill.

Todo Peru!

Moonlight Ride from mountaintop to distant valley

"Bill!" I shout, my head twisted backward in his direction, "Is it true about the brakes?"

"Yep."

"How do we stop?"

"Haven't you noticed the driver putting a rock behind the front tires? Don't worry," he says comfortingly. "We'll just go in low gear."

Tricia and I try to readjust our position for the downward tilt. If only I could get the corner of that box from under my spine. Judy is sliding in Tim's arms, thus causing Raul to slide into my slot, which pushes me into Tricia, who is wedged sideways against the side slats of the truck. I'm cold and exhausted and begin to shiver. Not even a hot flash from Tricia can help me now. Raul, lying on his back, looks up at the moon. He kisses his fingertips and reaches toward the sky.

Yo beso la luna.
Yo amo la luna.
Saludo a la luna
Que alumbra nuestro camino

....

I kiss the moon.
I love the moon.
I salute the moon
That lights our way

No wonder the Incas revered the sun and the moon. They are the main characters in the drama that is Peru.

Once again, we encourage Pat to join us. Brad entreats her to climb in with us where she'll be warmer. She still declines and remains shivering under a dripping poncho in the far corner of the truck.

"This is no time to be a martyr," Tricia remarks. Raul pulls the sleeping bag over me, Tricia, and himself and produces a small bottle of *trago* he bought by the side of the road at lunch. We giggle and snuggle closer, pulling the sleeping bag over our heads. Jokes rain down from above.

In a world that has become more real to me than any other, I relax in my nest of crates and smelly saddle blankets. I know the brakes won't give out, that we won't go over a cliff. It's not my destiny.

AT NINE O'CLOCK WE RATTLE OVER the cobblestones of Ollantaytambo. Bill suggests we stop at a café and give the driver a rest and some food. I forgot there were such things. We have been traveling for ten hours since we left Chaullay.

How strange to walk on level ground, sit in a chair at a table, and drink rum and Inca Cola from a glass. We could be sipping Campari and soda on the Via Veneto. Our driver stares at his plate of macaroni and green peppers, lifts his fork, and attacks with gusto.

I walk back to the kitchen to pay for our drinks and inquire about the toilet. The cook points a black stained finger to a small door that conceals a closet with a stinking hole in the floor—no moonlight, no quivering bushes, no rushing river. As I pass the kitchen and thank the *señora*, I notice the chickens and guinea pigs have retired to their corner by the stove.

Back in the truck, I am warm and happy and half asleep. The sky is clear, the moon bright but far away in a place I've left behind. Raul's hand appears on the other side of me, which must mean that his arm is around me. This is comforting. He whispers something in my ear about going dancing at the *Inca Huasi* tomorrow. His lips brush across my cheek as he whispers in my ear, "*Eres una mujer de mucho coraje.* (You are a woman of much courage.)" I think I just fell in love with him.

Rocked gently by the swaying motion of the truck on a smooth road, I am semiconscious of high mountains and eucalyptus trees flying by in the moonlight. I can see better with my eyes closed. Images fall one upon another—the glow of campfires, burros trotting under orange packs, rocky trails to be conquered, deep gorges and soaring snow-clad peaks. I feel such a deep sense of harmony in the simple elements of that world and that time that I long for the truck to slow down and not take it all away from me.

I want to hang on to the sounds of the rivers, the click of horses' hooves on granite, soft voices murmuring in Quechua, Raul's tinkling laugh, and the crash of a glacier. Instead, I hear cars honking. I want to cling to Raul, as if by hanging on to him, I can hang on to Peru.

The truck stops. I open my eyes and see bright lights where the stars should be. Telephone wires cross the night sky, and the moon is gone. A clean white wall with HOTEL LIBERTADOR printed in black letters is not the welcome sight I thought it would be—at least not yet.

With a wrenching screech, the gate of the truck is pulled down. We climb over packs and boxes and into the street. Bill comes out of the hotel and announces that there is plenty of room, showers, food. Philippe and Marilyn urge us to hurry. The dining room is closing. Dining room?

I say good-bye to Cerilio, Raul, and Jaime, as they fade into the shadows of the street and into memories of a time and place I will never forget.

Chapter Nineteen

HOME AGAIN IN CUSCO

▼▼▼▼▼▼▼▼▼▼▼▼▼▼▼

I n the morning, Cusco throbs with activity as we walk up the
Calle del Sol to the Plaza de Armas. Along the way, we stop
to greet the Indian women who look up at us from their piles
of weavings, pots, ponchos, rugs, and silver ornaments. They
remember us from a week ago, and when I tell them where we
have been, they nod their wise heads and say, "*Muy peligroso,
mamita, muy peligoso.* (Very dangerous, little mother.)" They tell
us they're glad we are home again.

Eager to join the natives from all over Peru who have come
to watch the parade that precedes tomorrow's celebration of Inti
Raymi, we continue up a crowded street that reeks of urine and
the familiar scent of eucalyptus smoke from the *anticucho* stands.
Today they are comforting, coming-home kinds of smells.

Judy joins us, and we make our way through the crush of deter-
mined celebrants. Stern policemen stand at the street corners, their
arms outstretched with a stick in each hand, trying to hold back the
swelling surge from the sidewalks into the streets. I grab a corner
of Tricia's jacket, hoping to stay linked until we reach the back
stairs of the Restaurant El Mesón, where Jaime has returned from

his "first vacation in fourteen years" to resume his job as maître d' of Cusco's finest restaurant. He greets each of us with a firm *abrazo*—not just any old nice-to-see-you-again *abrazo*, but a sincere and wholehearted hug like the ones we received every night on the trail when we straggled into camp and found Jaime and Raul setting up their kitchen. Jaime, darkly tanned now, white teeth to match the starched white shirt, leans forward and says, "*Tengo una mesa muy especial para mis mujeres.* (I have a very special table for my women.)"

He leads us through the restaurant, passing a table occupied by a contingent of older Peruvian men in coats and ties and women in proper city dresses.

"*Ní el vice presidente de la nacion puede tener esta mesa.* (Not even the vice president of the nation gets this table)," he says, nodding in their direction while guiding us to a table on the balcony overlooking the plaza.

"The vice president!" Judy exclaims, looking back at the group assembled in the center of the room.

Jaime returns with a tray of pisco sours, three bowls of chimichurri sauce (one made with mustard, one with oregano, one with onions and tomatoes—all with olive oil and garlic), and a basket of bread. After finishing all three varieties of chimichurri and four loaves of bread, we order lunch.

BAND AFTER CACOPHONOUS BAND, followed by groups of thirty to fifty men and women, enter the Plaza de Armas from a side street below our balcony. Jaime leaves the vice president's table and joins us to watch the parade.

"Each group represents an *allyu* (clan). They come from all the provinces of Peru," he tells us. A blur of ponchos encircles the plaza—red, purple, orange, gold, colors of the plants and the berries that grow in the highlands. What bliss—the view from the balcony, Cusco dancing below, pisco sours, and Jaime's loving care.

We've finished lunch, paid the bill, and are ready to leave, when Raul comes striding through the restaurant to our table. *"Vamos a bailar.* (Let's go dance)," he says. Kate and Tricia want no part of dancing in the street. "This is the perfect occasion for an attack by the Sendero Luminoso," Kate says.

I am torn. Should I return with my friends to the safety of the hotel or be an awkward third person?

"Go with Raul," I say to Judy.

"No, he wants us both," she replies.

"Yo amo las dos. (I love you both)," he says

Not exactly dragging my feet, I descend to the plaza with Judy and Raul and wave hesitantly at Kate and Tricia, as they give a thumbs-up and disappear into the crowd.

Raul puts one arm around Judy's shoulders and the other around mine, kisses each of us on the cheek, and guides us to the corner where the Calle del Sol meets the Plaza de Armas. Groups of dancers, momentarily camped while they wait their turn to approach the plaza, are lined up and down the middle of the street.

Holding hands, we weave our way down a side of the street, observing each group of musicians and dancers. Some sit sullenly by the chicha jug, chewing coca leaves and staring at the pavement. Others are more animated—laughing, shouting, arguing. Raul never lets either of us out of his sight. He says we should return to the plaza. People are getting restless, drinking too much. From the conversations on the street, he fears that fights might break out. He tells us that the government has banned the sale of alcohol in bars that are not in tourist hotels. Although the Sendero Luminoso "declared war" the day we left on our horseback trek, no one is really sure what they will do. Previous experience with terrorist groups has taught Peruvians to be wary wherever large crowds assemble. Raul has a healthy respect for this.

The familiar sound of *quenas*, *bombas*, and *zampoñas* playing a spirited *carnavalito* (a joyful, pre-Hispanic dance from the altiplano) comes from the plaza. Raul takes our hands, and we join locals, costumed dancers, and waltzing *charanquistas* (charango players) in a loose conga line that grows longer and louder as it encircles the square. Although there are moments when my chest feels like it will either explode or cave in, I realize I could not have done this when we arrived over a week ago. I could barely walk up the stairs of the hotel that first day. Now, I can dance around the square.

I remember the day we arrived in Cusco and witnessed a different parade from the steps of the cathedral. Then, we watched as tourists enjoying a colorful local event. Now, after the experiences of the last nine days, we feel we are part of the celebration.

Raul dances us down a street to our hotel, where he kisses us both goodnight and tells us both he loves us.

Chapter Twenty

INTI RAYMI

▼▼▼▼▼▼▼▼▼▼▼▼▼▼▼▼

Today is June 25, Inti Raymi, a day on which the Incas have
paid homage to *Apu Inti* (Lord Sun) every year since 1100 AD,
when Manco Capac founded the city of Cusco.

Bernardo Cobo, a Jesuit priest who arrived in Cusco in 1609,
and who was an accurate chronicler of Inca rituals, wrote in his
book *Historia del Nuevo Mundo*, "The Incas visualized the Sun in
their imagination as if it were a man, and consequently they said
the Moon was his wife and the stars their daughters." He also wrote
that the Incas believed that an eclipse "foretold the death of some
prince," and when that happened, they believed "the sun went into
mourning because he had nothing to do in the world."

My recent experiences in Peru have given me a profound
appreciation for the light and the warmth of the sun, and I have
observed the remains of temples to the sun in almost every town we
have visited—testimony that sun worship was revered and wide-
spread throughout the Inca Empire.

Although the fiesta doesn't begin until noon, Kate, Tricia, and
I join Bill, Lauren, and Judy in the hotel lobby at ten for the half-
hour walk up to Sacsayhuaman, the great Inca fortress on a plain
above Cusco.

We walk quickly through the town and up a path above a river to the ticket gate at the eastern end of the ruins. After claiming our seats in the wooden bleachers set at the far end of a rectangular field, we sit down to eat our picnic lunches and contemplate the surroundings.

A stone wall at least twenty feet high zigzags across the plain on my right. The polygonal pattern of the stones resembles a jumble of gigantic granite pillows sewn together with invisible seams, each one casting a shadow on its neighbor. Behind that forbidding wall, two more walls with slightly smaller stones follow the contours of the hill that rises above the plain. All three walls have more than twenty zigzags.

They were designed this way, Hemming says in *The Conquest of the Incas*, to force attacking armies to expose their flanks. *Who were the attackers?* I wonder, and I flip through my guidebook in search of an answer. There were no attackers until Manco Inca reclaimed the fort from the Spaniards in 1536 and began to attack the besieged Spaniards in Cusco with daily raids of fire and arrows. Chroniclers believe there were one to two hundred thousand Indians at Sacsayhuaman in May, when Juan Pizarro prepared to reclaim the fortress in an attack that would change the history of Peru.

With a cavalry of only fifty horsemen, Pizarro and his men fought through native barricades, navigated roads mined with hidden pits, and galloped up to a plateau above the city. From there, they attacked a series of outer barriers with Juan Pizarro leading the charge right up to the gate, where they were pelted with spears, rocks, and arrows. Pizarro, not wearing his helmet because of an injury to his jaw, was struck a mortal blow on his head and was removed secretly to Cusco, where he died at age twenty-five.

The following day, with his younger brother, Gonzalo, fighting off a large number of warriors on the hill across from the fort, the battle continued until night, when the Spaniards scaled the mighty terrace walls on ladders they had previously constructed.

Their supply of water, stones, and arrows dwindling, a large contingent of the defenders miraculously fought their way out of the fortress and through the Spanish line to plead for reinforcements at Manco Inca's camp at Calca in the Urubamba Valley.

After about three more days and nights of fierce fighting and much heroism on both sides, the Spaniards prevailed. At the end of the battle, they slaughtered the estimated fifteen hundred remaining Inca warriors inside their fortress, guaranteeing the end of the Inca Empire.

BILL OFFERS TO SAVE OUR SEATS while we explore the ruins. "Don't go too far," he warns. "Thousands of Peruvians and tourists will be pouring in for the next hour."

Judy, Tricia, and Lauren go in search of the 361-ton megalith at the end of one of the zigzags. Kate suggests we check out the scene in a field across from the ruins.

"Remember when Bill said we would have to sleep here with all the Indians?" she reminds me.

I look at the little clusters of men, women, children, and dogs, plus a few bundles of personal belongings, and try to imagine our Western camping gear as part of the scene.

We stop to watch a woman cooking potatoes in a little oven she has constructed out of dirt and stone. I ask her if I can take her picture, and she hands me a dusty potato.

"*Papa de la huerta, mamacita.* (Potato from the garden, little mother)," she says, her wide smile revealing three large teeth.

Kate tells me not to eat it, but I don't want to seem ungrateful, so I bite into the skin, dirt and all.

"*Muy bueno,*" I say, spitting out the dirt. More women have gathered to see what the "little mothers" are up to. They laugh and offer us more potatoes.

On our way back to the bleachers, we stop and sit on a rock carved like a throne. With a panoramic view of the great walls, we contemplate the many theories of who built Sacsayhuaman, when, and why.

"Perhaps it was a religious temple," Kate says. "I read somewhere that the zigzags represent lightning bolts. There was a god of lightning, you know, just like water, rain, and wind."

"Some people think the zigzags represent the teeth of the puma, something to do with Cusco being the rest of his body," I offer.

"Cieza de Leon, the Spanish chronicler, called this place the 'Storehouse of the Sun,'" Kate says. "The Incas were big on storehouses."

I stare at the stubborn walls, as if they might reveal their secrets. How many times and in how many places have we asked, "Why here? What for?" Why are there so many different theories on Inca history? Is it because they had no written history, and it was lost in the many oral versions? Is it because only the conquering Spaniards could record and interpret their history?

By the time we return to our seats, the bleachers are packed, and thousands of spectators have found a spot on every horizontal space that the zigzagging walls provide. Thousands more watch from the hills beyond the walls. A faux stone dais has been erected in the center of the field.

Slow, deliberate drumbeats sound as lines of women enter single file from the four corners of the square, symbolizing the four *suyos* of Tawantinsuyo—the Inca Universe. Walking slowly to the measured pace of the drumbeats, they bear offerings from their corresponding *suyo*: corn and potatoes carried on their heads or in outstretched arms, coca leaves in intricately woven bags, and chicha in clay jugs. Sweepers dart in and out, clearing their paths with branches of *retama* (scotch broom).

The protrusions of six gigantic zigzags in the surrounding

walls make dramatic points of entry for the groups that follow. The drums beat faster, and forty barefoot *chaskis* run swiftly around the field, followed by warriors with maces, clubs, shields, and arrows. Shirtless men jog into the field, their long black hair decorated with colorful headbands, feathers, fringes, and pointed leather helmets. A group of men carrying *chaki tacclas* (long wooden foot plows) on their shoulders take their place in the pageant.

When the square is filled with warriors, princesses, and feathered natives from the jungle provinces, a loud primeval blast from a conch shell announces the entrance of the great sun god, Inti, seated on a throne atop a litter carried by eight men. Their prominent cheekbones and slightly aquiline noses hint at true Inca ancestry— at least, that is what we have been told, that only true descendants are chosen to participate in this ceremony.

Inti steps down from his throne and climbs to the top of the dais, where he turns to his people and prays in Quechua for good crops. As he speaks into a microphone, his deep voice reverberates off the megalithic stones in front of him. He raises a bowl of chicha to the heavens, drinks, and gives the bowl to an attendant who has brought two llamas to be sacrificed.

Tricia and I are horrified and look away from the scene.

"Don't worry," Kate assures us. "They won't really kill them. They'll just stuff them down a hole under the platform."

"Actually," Bill says, "the high priest guys are supposed to examine the intestines and determine what will happen this coming year . . . not sure if they still do that."

Although I know that Inti Raymi has been researched by archeologists, historians, and Cusco event planners, and I respect their efforts to evoke the authentic Inca rituals of the past, I really don't want them to sacrifice those llamas.

"Do you think we should be thinking about how we're going to get out of here before all these thousands of people?" I ask Bill.

He scans the surrounding rocks and hills and suggests we make an early exit out of the bleachers and down to Cusco. Tricia and I ask if we can follow after we take some pictures.

Sensing that the celebration is coming to a close, I select a rock near one of the *suyos* with the sun at my back. I wait there for Inti to appear on his throne in my telephoto lens. He passes right in front of me, the plumes on his stave dancing in the wind and the sun glinting off a large medallion that covers his chest. The entire procession follows, and I click happily to the end of the roll.

Now I wonder where Tricia has gone. Thousands of Peruvians, tourists, and dancers are following the procession down the road to Cusco. I know the road is narrow with uneven stone steps, and I don't want to be caught there in the crush.

The lyrical notes of *quenas* beckon me to a flat area by one of the walls, where groups of dancers from the celebration are dancing with an urgency and abandon I've not witnessed on previous occasions. They are dancing for themselves, not for an audience. The women hold tambourines above their swirling braids, their fleet feet flitting beneath swirling skirts and petticoats. High-flying whips whir above their heads, as the *quenas* play faster, the drums beat louder, and I make my way to the protection of a wall and raise my camera.

No longer grouped by costume, by village, or by *ayllu*, the black hats fringed with strings of pearls are dancing with the plumed and feathered peaked hats. Younger men wear green-and-yellow-tasseled *chullos*, and they dance with everyone. Bare-chested bronze warriors wearing feathered headbands chase after the women wearing hats like plates with coins dangling in front of their eyes. Some have exquisitely embroidered ponchos.

Helmeted policemen stand close by in the shade of the walls, dwarfed by the gigantic stones. One of them approaches me.

"Are you looking for a friend?" he asks in English.

"Yes," I reply, wondering if Tricia has returned to Cusco without me.

"She is here," he says, leading me through the crowd to the exit.

"Oh, thank God I found you," Tricia says, thanking the young policeman in Spanish. "He told me to wait here while he went to look for you."

"I will walk with you now," he says. "There are many *ladrones* (thieves), pickpockets, and *gente mala* (bad people)."

I look over the sea of dark heads for likely suspects, put my camera away, switch my pack around to the front, cross my arms across my chest, and follow our escort down the stone stairway to the rocky road that leads straight into the heart of Cusco. There we bid our kind friend good-bye and return to the hotel to prepare for our farewell dinner at El Truco.

Chapter Twenty-One

FINAL FIESTA

▼▼▼▼▼▼▼▼▼▼▼▼▼

Tricia, Kate, and I arrive at the restaurant at nine. Kate's costume, fashioned from the streets and markets of Cusco, features an ancient manta in the faded reds of Andean dyes wrapped around her shoulders and held in place by a silver *tupu* depicting farmers planting corn. Handmade silver moons swing jauntily beneath her gray curls, and a woven sash is wrapped around her slightly diminished waist. She moves majestically, like a returning female warrior adorned with the spoils of war. Tricia and I follow humbly to our table of envious admirers.

Bill sits at the head of the long table by the dance floor, surrounded by the members of our group who went to Machu Picchu for the day—not the two days and a night as promised in our itinerary, but a lengthy day trip. The rest of us will do the same tomorrow. They shout their stories across the table over the amplified melody of the now-too-familiar "El Condor Pasa."

Through cupped hands, Brad yells, "We took the non-tourist train, and it left an hour early! Almost missed it. Luckily, Bill warned us and got us to the train station in time."

"It was worth it, though," Pat adds, "because we got there before all the tourists arrived and mobbed the place. But watch out for thieves in the train station. . . . Brad had a dollar bill stolen out of his shirt pocket that was buttoned. Don't know how they did that."

Jaime and his wife join us, followed by Raul, who seems more mischievous and animated than usual. He finds a chair and inserts it between Judy and me. While hugging one and kissing the other, he tells Kate that she is the most beautiful woman in the room. It is true that she has a certain radiance that we haven't seen for a while. How nice that Raul recognizes her inner beauty and says so without hesitation. Kate looks at him with a mixture of affection and medical scrutiny. "Where have you been all day?" she asks.

"Playing soccer, drinking beer," he says.

Musicians burst upon the stage, and the audience claps to the beat of a lively *marinera*. Raul takes my arm, grabs two napkins from a nearby table, hands me one, and lays the other on my shoulder as an invitation to follow him on to the dance floor. With white napkins spinning above our heads, we skip and hop in our own interpretation of this popular folk dance from the coast of Peru.

I learned a similar dance called *la Cueca* in Chile, but that was at sea level where physical exertion is barely noticed. Lively and flirtatious, the male dancer chases the girl while she coquettishly avoids him. Raul raises the art of flirting to Olympic level when he holds the napkin in two hands above my head, looks into my eyes, and breaks into an animated *zapateo* (foot-stomping tap dance).

I stand in front of him, waving my napkin around his stamping feet, hoping to catch my breath, but too soon we're whirling about the room again. My heart pounds, head spins . . . must keep dancing . . . I'm in love with Peru, the music, the people, Raul, Jaime—all of it!

We collapse in our chairs. Perspiration drips from Raul's chin, and Kate reaches across the table to take his pulse.

"I'm just checking to see if it's true that people who live above eleven thousand feet really have a greater lung capacity," she says.

I stare at my pisco sour, too breathless to speak or to drink. Tomorrow, Kate, Tricia, and I will go to Machu Picchu—once the climax of our trip—now, it seems, the anticlimax. I vow to return and give that fabled site the time and attention it deserves.

I turn to Kate and Tricia and say, "Hey, do you want to come back next year and hike the Inca Trail to Machu Picchu?"

"Oh, my God," Tricia says. "There you go planning the next trip when this one isn't even over."

Around and across the table, we recount the *best moments*—the top of the pass at Salcantay, the hot springs, returning safely to Ollantaytambo in the Urubamba Valley—and the *worst* ones—Kate's fall, no train in Santa Teresa, the long march to Chaullay. For me, I think, the best and the worst have become one and the same.

We raise our glasses in a final tribute to having "made it" over the Andes (twice) and up the river and back to Cusco by horse and by foot and by truck. Just like the Incas when they returned to Cusco from their great conquests, we celebrate ours with "much feasting and rejoicing."

The treasures we have found in Peru are as good as Inca gold.

ACKNOWLEDGMENTS

▼▼▼▼▼▼▼▼▼▼▼▼▼▼▼

First on my list is, and always will be, my husband, Osvaldo, who opened the door for me to Latin America—its culture, its language, and its magnificent scenery. Our honeymoon from San Francisco to Valparaíso by ship, then over the Andes and across Patagonia by car to his home in Bariloche was our first of many adventures in a land of infinite possibilities. Now you can stop saying to me, "Go write that book!"

Thank you, Bill Roberson, for enticing me and my friends at a slide show in my home, then guiding us (more or less) from Cusco to Salcantay, down rivers and up mountains until we reached the very top, where you threw off a plastic tarp, stood on top of the truck, spread your arms and exclaimed to us huddling passengers, "This is Todo Perú!"

After seeing the slides of Perú my good friends, Joan Klaussen and Vicki Johnson, wondered—Perú? Why not? Having raised children, owned and managed businesses, we were ready for a trip free of family responsibilities—something slightly adventurous, foreign, and physically challenging. Joan and Vickie, soulmates and tent-mates, now deceased, made the whole adventure worth writing this book.

In Cusco, Hugo Paullo and his son, Angel, introduced us to their land and their Inca legacy, as they guided us from ruins to remote villages, over the Andes and into the jungle. They were more than guides—co-conspirators in a grand adventure, friends forever. *Gracias, queridos compañeros.*

I might not have written this book if Dick Reinhardt hadn't mentioned non-fiction travel narrative as an actual genre, and I wouldn't have known how to write it without workshops, panels, and friendships I've made through the Squaw Valley Community of Writers. Thank you Louis Jones, Molly Giles, and Julie Siler for reading early versions and cheering me on.

Larry Habegger—writer, teacher, editor, publisher—he has done it all and for many years. How fortunate I was to attend his non-fiction workshop in San Francisco in 2011, where Larry's logical edits and thoughtful comments transformed my first six chapters and made me think more deeply about the rest of the book.

When the Book Passage, beloved haven for Bay Area readers and writers, announced a program called 'Path to Publishing', I signed up, wrote a proposal, and sent it to Don George. What followed was a six-month journey, almost as great as the story itself; as Don sent me searching for a better word, a more meaningful phrase, a more precise description. Don made me dig deeper, try harder, think longer, and ultimately become a better writer. There are no words that adequately express my gratitude for his guidance and his friendship.

Marcos, Carmen, and René, my brave and trusting children, thank you for following me to Perú, to Salcantay, along the Inca trail and on many of my life's best journeys. And thank you for reminding me, "Mom, you can do anything. You hiked the Inca Trail twice."

Thanks to my sister-in-law, Alexandra Starr, who gave me Evelyn Kohl LaTorre's memoir, *Between Inca Walls*, where I discovered the publisher, She Writes Press.

Thank you, Brooke Warner, Samantha Strom, and She Writes Press, for providing a path to publishing for many fine writers, and for the support and expertise of your copy editors, design, sales and production team.

Cheryl McLaughlin coached me through the labyrinth of social media, prodding and proposing her creative marketing schemes, while guiding me with humor and respect for my age. Her technical expertise and background in Sport Psychology are essential elements of a successful publicity campaign.

ABOUT THE AUTHOR

Eddy Ancinas grew up in the San Francisco Bay Area and on a nearby cattle ranch. A non-fiction writer specializing in Latin American travel, she has published articles on Argentina, Chile, and Peru in the *San Francisco Chronicle*, *Boston Globe* and *LA Times,* plus six editions of *Fodor's Argentina Guide.* Her story of a cattle roundup in Elko, Nevada, won the 2010 Nevada Magazine Writers' Contest. Her award-winning book on the history of two ski areas (now one: Alpine Meadows and Palisades-Tahoe), *Tales from Two Valleys: Squaw Valley and Alpine Meadows,* was first published in 2013; a 2nd edition came out in 2019. Eddy has an Argentine husband and is fluent in Spanish.

SELECTED TITLES FROM SHE WRITES PRESS

She Writes Press is an independent publishing company founded to serve women writers everywhere. Visit us at www.shewritespress.com.

Bowing to Elephants: Tales of a Travel Junkie by Mag Dimond. $16.95, 978-1-63152-596-4. Mag Dimond, an unloved girl from San Francisco, becomes a travel junkie to avoid the fate of her narcissistic, alcoholic mother—but everywhere she goes, she's haunted by memories of her mother's neglect, and by a hunger to find out who she is, until she finds peace and her authentic self in the refuge of Buddhist practice.

Brave(ish): A Memoir of a Recovering Perfectionist by Margaret Davis Ghielmetti. $16.95, 978-1-63152-747-0. An intrepid traveler sets off at forty to live the expatriate dream overseas—only to discover that she has no idea how to live even her own life. Part travelogue and part transformation tale, Ghielmetti's memoir, narrated with humor and warmth, proves that it's never too late to reconnect with our authentic selves—if we dare to put our own lives first at last.

Finding Venerable Mother: A Daughter's Spiritual Quest to Thailand by Cindy Rasicot. $16.95, 978-1-63152-702-9. In midlife, Cindy travels halfway around the world to Thailand and unexpectedly discovers a Thai Buddhist nun who offers her the unconditional love and acceptance her own mother was never able to provide. This soulful and engaging memoir reminds readers that when we go forward with a truly open heart, faith, forgiveness, and love are all possible.

Reclaiming Home: Diary of a Journey Through Post-Apartheid South Africa by Lesego Malepe. $16.95, 978-1-63152-332-8. Malepe documents her travels in South Africa in 2004, the 10th anniversary of South Africa's democracy—a sprawling, revealing journey that illuminates the ways South Africa has changed, and the ways it has remained the same, since the end of apartheid.

She Rode a Harley: A Memoir of Love and Motorcycles by Mary Jane Black. $16.95, 978-1-63152-620-6. After escaping an abusive marriage, Mary Jane finds love with Dwayne, who teaches her to ride a Harley; traveling together, they learn to be partners, both on and off the road, until Dwayne gets cancer. Without him, Mary Jane once again must learn to live on her own—but she'll never be the same again.